"Beautifully written, extraordinarily insightful, unsparing, relentless, and radical in its furious desire to lay bare the truth of a family tragedy."

—MICHAEL IGNATIEFF
Historian, novelist, past leader of Canada's Liberal Party,
currently Rector and President of Central European University

"Paul Kahn bears *Testimony* to the pain and helplessness of dealing with a loved one whose psyche is damaged and whose inner world is intractably hardened against persuasion. This thoughtful saga of frustration and vulnerability is an honest and vivid depiction of suffering which affects not only the sufferer but everyone who loves, and thus is unable either to help or to flee a relentless cycle of illusory hope and crushing despair. *Testimony* advocates no traditional remedies, yet faith is crucially important. For Kahn, who lacks religious rituals, faith 'without myth is love,' a way of being in the world expressed, not by arguments but by actions. Kahn writes persuasively and beautifully, 'I call my faith love.'"

—MARGARET R. MILES
Author of *Recollections and Reconsiderations*

"Paul Kahn's *Testimony* is an extraordinary and profound meditation on the fundamental questions of human existence—trauma, rage, memory, love, faith, and care—drawn from a shattering struggle of a son with his father's life. It is a testimony as well to Kahn's unique combination of philosophical brilliance and astute human understanding."

—MOSHE HALBERTAL
New York University School of Law

"War and trauma, sex and betrayal, memory and truth, faith and authenticity—Kahn's struggle to make sense of his mother's late-life confession of adultery and his father's endless rage lead him on a journey into the marrow of existence. This is not merely a memoir, but an offering, one that is unfailingly honest but not brutally so, probing but never voyeuristic; Kahn redeems the tragedy of his parents' lives by attending to them in both their high drama and their prosaic mundanity, by affirming that they matter, that he cares. It is also, by the same token, a confession, an act of faith, a declaration that since love is real, it is possible to live in the face of death. What sort of religious act is possible for one bereft of tradition, ritual, and myth? In *Testimony*, Kahn has shown us."

—JENNIFER A. HERDT
Yale Divinity School

Testimony

Testimony

Paul W. Kahn

CASCADE *Books* • Eugene, Oregon

TESTIMONY

Cascade Books
An Imprint of Wipf and Stock Publishers
199 W. 8th Ave., Suite 3
Eugene, OR 97401

www.wipfandstock.com

PAPERBACK ISBN: 978-1-7252-8430-2
HARDCOVER ISBN: 978-1-7252-8431-9
EBOOK ISBN: 978-1-7252-8432-6

Cataloguing-in-Publication data:

Names: Kahn, Paul W., author.

Title: Testimony / Paul W. Kahn.

Description: Eugene, OR : Cascade Books, 2021.

Identifiers: ISBN 978-1-7252-8430-2 (paperback) | ISBN 978-1-7252-8431-9 (hardcover) | ISBN 978-1-7252-8432-6 (ebook)

Subjects: LCSH: Kahn, Paul W., 1952–. | Kahn, Paul W., 1952– —Biography. | Philosophers—United States—Biography.

Classification: B851 .K34 2021 (print) | B851 .K34 (ebook)

02/05/21

For Suzanne and Hannah,
who should know the story of their grandparents.

Contents

Acknowledgments

In these pages, I tell the story of my parents from my point of view. My brother Gary and my sister Karen make occasional appearances in that story. Before I begin, I want to acknowledge that they, no doubt, have their own stories to tell about this family. They too have had to bear the burden of my parents' life and, particularly, of their final years of struggle.

Truth

On my mother's seventy-fifth birthday, she began to confess. By her eightieth birthday, she was dead. In those five years, my parents' quiet life in retirement became the scene of a battle of mythic proportions. Love and hatred, sex and possession, memory and truth, life and death were all at issue. How can I explain this? Could she, a secular Jew, have discovered the mystery of confession? Was she constructing her own last rites? Where did she get her deep belief that speaking the truth would put things right with whomever it is that we have to put things right? In my mother's case, that was not God but my father.

My father, who thought of himself as even less of a Jew than my mother, had nothing at all of the Christian penchant for forgiveness. He was what we now call an "evangelical atheist." His response to my mother's confession was not mercy but violent rage. Words of forgiveness simply were not in his vocabulary. If he was to be God to this act of confession, he was going to be a vengeful God. Not a glimmer of "love your enemy"; no belief that "the truth shall set you free." For him, it was the righteous violence of Jehovah all the way—except what looks like justice from an offended God looked like evil when coming from my father.

If there were any priest at hand, someone to mediate between the sinner's confession and the possibility of redemptive grace, it would have been me. Unfortunately, I had no such powers. I could not transform pain into sacrifice for either of them. I could not forgive her sin or make his world whole again. I could not even call a truce. I was like a priest who

1

has lost his faith: one who remembers the words of ritual but no longer believes there is anything behind them. Whatever I might say to try to reassure either of them, I did not really believe it. What I thought was that their world had fallen apart and there was no possibility of repair or of rescue. They were locked in a struggle without end—a struggle that neither of them could walk away from and neither could win. A struggle to the death, which is exactly what happened.

Whatever priestly function I can serve comes now: to tell the tale and preserve the memory. Why remember this tale of pain without redemption? Because here there was life, the thing itself. It showed itself with a brute force that stripped away every excuse and every diversion. In their struggle, there was no polite holding back, no therapeutic intervention, no shifting of attention onto the labor of career and family. There was only the intensity of the struggle, consuming everything and everyone that got in its way. All who entered their little world felt they were in the presence of something real, extraordinary, and terrible. This was the *mysterium tremendum* of the ancient gods: at once awesome and terrifying.

Perhaps you will think that this is my own confession, but I do not feel my mother's need to come clean with anyone. I prefer to think of this as testimony. I was a witness. I must say what I saw. More than that, I must say what I felt, for this is not a story of action but of hearts opened and broken. If we are to make any sense of our lives, we must understand that the sources of evil in the human heart are exactly the same as the sources of love. All that is of lasting significance occurs at the extremes. There, we learn who we are. We learn whether we have a faith that can support sacrifice or a hatred that can support murder. We learn that for every act of love, there is the threat of a corresponding act of evil. My parents brought themselves to this extreme where love could not be easily separated from evil. They were bound to each other in love and in hatred. That was the fact. Neither could imagine life without the other. That hardly meant that they were at peace with each other.

No one comes out of this story happy. There is no point of closure where all is resolved in mutual forgiveness. Not even death brought them to closure. Both were looking for a blessing that could release them from what they could not bear. Unfortunately, there was none to be had. Each wanted to hear from the other "you are my all"; each managed to hear only "you are nothing to me." Love will draw you in, but it can leave you with hate. Maybe only love can do that, for one must really care to hate. Who is more dangerous than the passionate believer is? Think of the soldier who simultaneously practices a murderous hatred and a sacrificial love. Opposites tend to merge at the extremes: in politics, the far right and far left; in literature, comedy and tragedy; in life, love and hate.

The ancient texts tell us that sin is inevitable. That much they certainly got right. They also tell us that there is hope for redemption from a caring God. This is much harder to believe today. We are on our own. We are, however, not without resources. If we cannot rely upon a caring God, we can still care for each other. Love or hatred? That is the question with which my parents struggled. It is no less a question for all of us who follow.

My parents' story is, in parts, unbearably painful. In other parts, it is comic. It is a story as much about the destruction and the promise of the twentieth century as it is about the unchanging character of the human soul. It begins for my father in the Great Depression, and for my mother in Hitler's Germany. It ends in suburban Connecticut. In between, there is the war in Europe and the cultural revolution of the sixties; there is corporate America and the escape to rural America. It is most of all the oldest story that we have, that of love and betrayal, with everything moving inexorably toward death. Like any great drama, their story links the timeless and the timely.

In the Bible, we learn that Israel was the new name given to Jacob after he wrestled all night with God on his return to Canaan. What kind of people struggle with their God instead of bowing down in worshipful respect? Perhaps one that finds faith itself to be a struggle; one that worries that faith may mean a loss of freedom. If the claim of God upon his chosen people is whole and complete, can there be any freedom that is not idolatry? It sometimes seems that every free act by the Israelites was also an act of idolatry. The ancient writers often referred to the relationship of the Jews to their God as if it were a marriage. They appealed to the metaphor of adultery to describe the failure of the Israelites to keep the covenant. Adultery and idolatry are both world-destroying; both destroy the faith upon which a life is built.

Today, for many of us, the direction of the metaphor has reversed. The faith that is real is that of love; the act of betrayal is not idolatry, but adultery. Of love, we ask the same question that was once asked of faith: If the claim of love is whole and complete, where is freedom? Must the free act look like betrayal? Does it create a new idol? That was surely how my father responded to my mother's confession.

Can we have both autonomy—the quintessential modern virtue— and love—the most traditional of all values? If we must choose, what is it to be? If we cannot decide, are we left only with the struggle? My parents were locked in a struggle that began with a free act of betrayal; it sustained itself only through a faith that kept them bound to each other. Neither of them could walk away, but neither could they stop fighting.

Just as idolatry makes sense only in a world of believers, there can be no betrayal unless there is a love to be betrayed. It requires a kind of faith to see in the sexual act a world-destroying betrayal. This is particularly true today, when sex has been brought into the public sphere as if it were an ordinary commodity. My mother confessed an act of adultery; my father saw an act of idolatry. He could no more forgive this than could God forgive the Israelites their turn to a golden calf.

The pain of betrayal is an ache in the universe of meaning that constitutes our lives. We must already have staked our all on each other, if we care so deeply about betrayal. We see the same thing with political betrayal. Treason is a crime only for a member of our community. The stranger may commit the same act with the same damage, but it is not treason. It may not even be a crime. We do not care about the sexual act until there is love. But once there is love, that act carries all the old power of idolatry. On such a frail thing—an act or an idol—are whole worlds built and destroyed.

Idolatry loses its force when faith becomes a purely individual matter. There is no one to judge the direction of your faith, then, for we are no longer accountable to each other in our religious practices and beliefs. I can be indifferent to the question of the existence of your gods. Adultery, too, becomes a matter of indifference once love becomes only a private feeling. We are not accountable to each other for our feelings. To care about the sexual act, we must care about our mutual world. That mutual world is what love creates and sustains.

My parents thought about none of this. They had no faith in the Jewish God or in any other. Neither was given to reflections on religion, faith, or history. Nevertheless, the patterns of meaning that direct our actions and make sense of our world are bred deep in the bone. They form a common language behind our many differences. My parents could no more escape the Western religious inheritance than they could escape the modernism of the twentieth century. Locked in a world-shattering struggle, they knew that, even with all of its pain, this was where they belonged. It was their fate, even if they had brought it upon themselves. There was nothing to be done, except to live out their lives. They would do so even if it meant destroying each other and terrifying everyone who came near them. They could see no exit apart from death. Neither could I.

Nothing had prepared me for my mother's confession. She had always been a talkative person, but hardly confessional. She was not given to self-reflection—or so I thought. Her talk was mostly chatter, banter about the day, the neighbors, and the relatives. Serious conversation about herself or anything else was not of much interest to her. She really had no idea what her philosopher son thought about. The question just did not cross her mind. Enough that he had taught her nephew's child or that her neighbor had once seen a poster advertising a lecture he was giving. Her real passion was "Jewish geography," which is the Jewish equivalent of the Mormons' pursuit of genealogy. Because Jews have spent so much time fleeing from one place to another, our family trees tend to become maps. We need to know where the aunts, uncles, and cousins are, just in case we have to go somewhere fast. Once, driving home from college, I was caught in a blizzard outside of Cleveland, Ohio. Sure enough, a call to my mother located a distant cousin living close by—Jewish geography at work.

She liked to read, and she talked about the books that she was reading. Her tastes ran toward book-club fiction and that genre of late twentieth-century Jewish memoir that often seems the only sort of book reviewed in the Sunday papers. Apparently, my mother was not alone in her reading habits. A refugee from Hitler's Germany, she was always interested in reading about how others had managed the transition from old Europe to New York. She identified with them—less because they had fled Europe than because they, too, had grown up in the City.

She was not particularly interested in the Holocaust itself, although most of her extended family was lost. I am sure she never read a history of twentieth-century Germany. Weimar meant nothing to her. Europe was only a map of scattered relatives: a couple in Paris, a few in Luxembourg, and then a few more here and there in small towns along what had been the periphery of the Reich. Her world began when, at age 11, she arrived in New York. She liked to tell us that she had had her birthday on the boat, just as it was arriving. That was, for her, a moment of rebirth, of beginning again. How she got there was a story about aunts and uncles, not about the great movement of twentieth-century history. For reasons unknown to me, the survivors in our family all seem to have come west. She never went to Israel and never spoke of relatives there. She never spoke of it at all. If it did not show up on the family tree, it was not on the map as far as she was concerned.

My mother could not stand silence. When no one was speaking, she would fill the void. Even that does not quite capture what was at stake, for she was not very good at listening. She did not have a longing for conversation in the sense of sustained discussion. For her, talking was broad but not deep. Ideally, her conversation would cover the globe. It would hold together the whole of the world. It was always in movement from one point to another, rarely settling anywhere for long. Listening to my mother was the verbal equivalent of standing in Times Square: eventually, just about everyone would pass by.

Her friends were not people with whom she pursued a single conversation over many years. Rather, they were opportunities for more talk. She was not using anyone or treating anyone unfairly. As far as I could tell, many of her friends seemed to have the same need for this sort of talk. They certainly seemed to enjoy it. I thought of them as like ants, mutually rubbing their antennae together. Talking, they sent out beacons of life to each other. "I am here, are you there?" All they wanted to hear was "yes." The rest was incidental.

My mother was not talking out of some sort of fear of the emptiness of silence itself. She had no need of background noise just to keep her mind occupied. This was not a household in which the television was on all the time. Music would not do either. The silence she could not stand was her own. She needed to talk. Speaking was an affirmation of living. "I speak, therefore I am" was the principle by which she lived. One of my very last images of her is in the hospital with a breathing tube down her throat. That must have been the most terrible moment of her life. I could see the absolute panic she felt. Her mouth was taped shut around the tube. "I am not" was the message in her eyes.

When other people were talking, she saw it not so much as a conversation as a series of prompts: each statement would elicit a response. If the speaker had an uncle who was ill, then my mother would have to tell of an aunt who was even sicker. There was an edge of competition in both the triumphs (read: children and grandchildren) and tragedies (read: illnesses). Tragedy and joy could follow each other in such rapid succession that one would lose track. Of course, the point was not to keep track, but just to keep talking.

Long ago, I stopped going to the movies with my mother. It was just too embarrassing. It was bad enough that she would keep talking through the credits. "Is he the actor that was in that movie we saw last year? Did they really make this in Rome?" The transition to silence was always a difficult process for her. It took her a while to realize that I was no longer responding to her questions. Worse, she never quite made it all the way to silence. There would be a recurrent chatter of commentary throughout the movie. She would ask herself little questions and immediately answer them. She would summarize the plot development and predict the next move just at the moment that it became obvious to everyone. "He's going to shoot her." Some sort of filter that most of us have between thought and speech was not engaging for her. Pretty soon, those around us would be going "shh." After a while, so would I.

The line between talking to herself and talking to others was just not very strong for her. This meant that the line between fact and fiction was also not very strong. The older she got, the weaker this line became. She had never been a reliable witness, but she was even less reliable when she was talking of the distant past. She would report on events that I was sure had never happened. Sometimes, they would involve me, and my memory is not yet that bad. She would report things I did as an adolescent that not only did not happen, but were impossible even to imagine happening. She would say that she was repeating something I had said, but would use words that I never use. The same was true of her reports on my siblings. Strikingly, there were never any other witnesses to what seemed to her important events in the life of our family. She simply made this stuff up, but she repeated it so often that it all seemed undeniably true to her. She had the support of all that endless testimony—her own.

I do not mean to suggest that her chatter was frivolous gossip or mere imaginings. She certainly was not above gossip, but she was not frivolous. She had no interest in movie stars or other celebrities. She did not watch *Oprah* or *Entertainment Tonight*. Actually, she did not watch much television at all. She had no interest, since there was no opportunity for verbal interaction. Watching and listening were not what she enjoyed. She was not interested in living vicariously through the rich and famous. She was not talking mindlessly about the weather, shopping, or fashion. Her talk was usually about things that were important to her: family and friends. That her talk seemed to get ahead of her thought was because she was always rushing into the future. She wanted to make sure that she did not miss anything and that no one missed her.

Nor do I mean to suggest that she spent her entire life chatting with friends and neighbors. She had a long career in social services. She did not just like to talk, she was also skilled with words in a professional way. She liked to be with people and she liked to do things for them. She had considerable organizational skills. She ran an office; she traveled the country. Children do not really know much about their parents' professional life, but my guess is that she ran her office in the same way that she carried on at home. There must have been an endless stream of chatter from her, directed at the people with whom she worked or the clients she served. This would not have kept her from also attending to their needs. Mostly, it would have felt welcoming and open. It was just her way of being with others. Imagine a doctor whose bedside manner is to fill the silence with talk. I have noticed the same quality in some dental hygienists: once I am caught in the chair with my mouth stretched open, they set into an endless monologue ranging from the weather, to their weekend plans, to the doings of their families. Still, I do get my teeth cleaned. That must have been my mother at work.

My father often made fun of her tendency toward ceaseless talk. She would, he believed, speak without forethought or reflection. She seemed confident in what she was saying, but only because she did not consider the alternatives. "Rarely right, but never uncertain" was his characterization. He used it often. He illustrated this with a funny story of when he was a law student, contesting a violation in traffic court. My mother was testifying confidently. The problem was that in describing the event, she was making up distances that supported the other side. My father told his lawyer to ask her how long a car was. She immediately answered, "about 50 feet," which was the end of her credibility as a witness. She remained the same even as she got older. She would confidently call out directions—"Go right"—but really she had no idea of where we were or where we were going. After a while, I just stopped listening. She did not seem to mind.

I believed this story my father told of my mother in court. At least, my mother never denied it. To me, it meant that her need to talk was not a habit of old age. It ran deep within her. It was what people remembered about her. She would strike up a conversation with anyone. The car story was not just about talk, however. It pointed to a deeper disorientation in the world. It was about directions and measures. She was not good with any kind of directions, from maps to recipes. She did not have the patience for them. She would move forward before she registered what to do next.

She would carelessly substitute one ingredient for another when cooking. She would confuse teaspoons for tablespoons or sugar for salt. It was not that she was following her own intuition of what was right. She was simply moving forward. She did not enjoy the process of preparation. She wanted to get to the table where talk had its proper forum. This was how she drove as well. She paid little attention to what was around her. She had a habit of running into stationary objects. I thought this was because things moving—other cars or pedestrians—knew enough to get out of the way. She gave off plenty of signals in her driving that you should indeed get out of the way. She had no interest in the traveling, but wanted only to get to her destination where she could pick up the conversation.

My mother liked everyone, but somehow she was not at ease in the world. I mean this literally. She just did not know what to do with her body. Sports were out of the question for her. She could not orient herself in space. She joked that she only passed physical education class in college because she did well on the written exam. She lacked coordination. Even going for a walk could be dangerous. She could trip over anything. More often than not, she would trip or run into something because she was too busy talking to pay attention to where she was putting her feet. She had to walk on solid ground, better paved than unpaved. A walk in the woods could be deadly. The world for her was created and sustained in talk. The rest was just obstacles.

The point was always to move forward. Yet she was not one to plan, or even to look, ahead. These were dangerous habits, as she got older. I spent a lot of time worrying that she would fall and break a hip. She came very close more than once. For some reason, the area around swimming pools was a particular danger zone. Maybe it was just that this was where the elderly would gather to talk in the summer and it had the particular disadvantage of not being carpeted—nothing to break her fall. I suspect as well that the fact that many conversations were going on at once among different clusters of people would disorient her. She would not know where to go, as she tried to hear what was going on everywhere. Once she tripped over a piece of pool furniture and cracked her jaw. Even with it wired shut and her food intake limited to what she could get through a straw, she did not stop talking. Another time, she tripped on the concrete apron of the pool. I rushed her to the emergency room, thinking that this time it really was the hip. She spent a few days in a wheel chair, but there was no break. No serious interruption in her conversation.

Where did this deep need to talk come from? I imagine it started with that brief period between when she arrived in New York and when she learned to speak English. I know from travels with my own children how terrible it is for a child not to understand anything that is going on around her because of the absence of language. My mother must have felt the collapse of her world. She was too young to understand the meaning of being a refugee, but old enough to feel a crisis of disorientation in the loss of language. She could not understand anything and she could not speak her feelings. Unable to express herself, exiled from her home, she must have felt as if she were both lost and invisible.

She learned English quickly and well. She was proud of the fact that she had no German accent, unlike her slightly older neighbor, Henry Kissinger. Even without the accent, however, her language bore the signs of this transition for the rest of her life. Her ceaseless talk was her accent; it was her distinctive approach to language. It was as if she never made up for that brief interlude when her lack of English effectively compelled her silence. She carried around that deficit forever. Once she recovered language, she was not going to be invisible. "I am here" was always the underlying message. Even toward the end, when she moved from chatter to confession, this was the truth of the message she endlessly conveyed to my father.

I could not think of my mother's ceaseless talk without thinking of the countless Jews who went silently to their deaths in the concentration camps. Like my mother, they had been forced out of their homes and communities. Many, I imagine, did not know the language of their oppressors, who refused to listen to them. A great, stunned silence proclaimed the loss of their world. My mother's incessant "I am here" spoke for all of them. It was her version of "never again."

Conversation between my parents moved in two different directions: she would chatter; he would declare. They would rarely meet in the middle. Each was talking at, rather than with, the other. She did not really expect anyone, including my father, to respond to her as if she were in a dialogue. She would have seen such a response as an interruption. She was occupying space through talk and wanted to take over as much as possible. So did he—not, however, through chatter. He would try to occupy all the space by excluding every possible position but his own. He would declare her wrong. He would say she was "talking nonsense." But then, in his view, so was almost everyone else. He had trouble with disagreement, quickly losing patience and declaring his interlocutor an "idiot." My mother was never defeated by this. She did not take his declarations seriously, any more than he took her endless talk seriously.

Just as neither of them was much of a listener, neither had much patience. They did not know how to wait. My mother was always rushing forward. My father would decide, and that would be the end of the matter as far as he was concerned. She, however, would lose track of what he had decided. She went her own way and usually pulled him along, for he had nowhere else to go. He would complain; he would say that the parties and dinners to which she dragged him were "torture time." Still, the two of them were inseparable.

Their conversation may not have found a common ground, but they did. They married just after the War. They raised three children. They moved around, but they remained together for decades—right up to her death. They were in many ways opposite personalities, but they learned to fit together. They knew that they complemented each other. She was a social person; he was not. My mother talked in order to make connections; my father talked to break them. Her chatter was a way of being with others; his declaring was a way of excluding others. She knew how to maintain the social fabric of their lives; he alienated most everyone. Without her, he might have withdrawn from the world. Without him, she might have been totally lost in the world. He knew where they were at every moment, but feared the future. She rushed into the future, paying little attention to where they were. They pushed and pulled at each other, and in that way stayed together.

My father could not have put his dependence upon my mother into words. He never gave up the idea that he did not need others, mortal or divine. He had no close friends. Actually, he barely had any distant friends. I cannot remember a single visit with or to friends of his. No college classmates, no war buddies, no colleagues from work. He had her.

My father had nothing but scorn for those with faith of any sort. This was unfortunate, not so much for him as for her. She would really have enjoyed the social life of a temple. She certainly could have used the support in the end. The temple, however, was the one place into which she could not pull him. He would not hear of it. Those with faith were all "idiots." Rabbis were absolutely at the bottom of his scale of humanity.

There is a family story that his bar mitzvah was derailed when he gave the rabbi a list of questions. I imagine those questions went to the existence of God and truth of the Old Testament story of the Jews. The rabbi failed this test and my father refused to go forward with the ceremony.

"There is no God," my father would declare, and that was the end of the matter. My mother had no faith that could stand against his militant atheism. I once asked her if she believed in God. She replied, "I believe in nature." I wondered how anyone could not believe in nature. I was not thinking of my father, who had no beliefs at all.

There was always about my father a barely suppressed anger. Indeed, when he was younger, it was not so suppressed. He would explode, storming about the house, banging doors, ripping up clothing, and all the while screaming. I learned to keep my head down, since it was entirely possible that things would start flying. After I came to realize that I was probably not going to be hit by anything, I tended to frame his outbursts as somehow heroic. I thought that he just could not stand the regimentation of corporate life or that he was in rebellion against suburban culture. It was the 1960s and rebellion could be the answer to many questions. Now, I do not make excuses for him. Fundamentally, his expectations for himself were larger than his accomplishments. He might declare, but not a lot of people were listening. Eventually, he got things into balance, but only by giving up his expectations. He no longer expected there to be any relationship between intelligence and success. These changed expectations did not lessen his resentment of the way things were.

Whatever it was that produced my father's youthful rage, I did not think then, and I do not think now, that it had much to do with my mother. She was often the immediate object of his wrath, but mostly he was just looking for an excuse to explode. No one could really get that angry over a missing button or an overcooked steak. For these things, you do not destroy. My mother knew that she was not the point of it all. She would wait for his fits of anger to pass; they always did. Usually the waiting included more chatter, only now shallow and under her breath. She meant for him to not quite hear what she was saying, but still to know that she was not silent. For her, it was always talk or die.

That my mother, at seventy-five, was striking up conversations at every opportunity was hardly new. That her talk turned from chatter to confession was entirely new. A person without religious faith, she found her confessors wherever she could. She would confess to friends, relatives, and acquaintances. It seemed as if she would confess to strangers, if they would only listen to her long enough. Worst of all, she confessed to my father. She did so over and over. She could not stop. This was no longer chatter. It was serious—deadly serious—talk. And he was listening. The old form of endless talk remained, but the content was now of an entirely different dimension. Imagine being accustomed to the chatter of an elderly person and then suddenly one day you stop and listen. You find that he is confessing to genocide in his youth. What do you do? Imagine that members of your family had been among his victims.

A close friend of mine, reflecting on his sixtieth birthday, told me "it focuses the mind." My mother's mind became very focused on her seventy-fifth birthday. Despite all that endless talk, something had not been said. The secret of her past had to be revealed. But as I just said, my mother was not a reliable witness on the deep past. I had to wonder whether she was making up her own past, just as she had made up mine. I still wonder. Once again, there were no other witnesses. Could it be that the entire drama of those last years was based on something that never happened? It could indeed, but it does not really matter. Just as my father's old angers had rested on something deeper than my mother's missteps, her confession rested on something deeper than her own sin. That she needed to confess was a fact; whether she was confessing to a fact remains unknown. For her, it was all the same. She really did believe that she had had the affair. She certainly convinced my father and he was the only listener who really mattered.

There is only one thing that moves us to confession: betrayal. For some, that betrayal is of God's commands. We confess our sins to God. Since they could not have been a secret to Him, the point cannot be to inform. Nor can confession be about punishment. God certainly need not wait for our confession to do His justice. If confession is not about bringing truth and justice into line, what is its point?

There is always a narrative line to confession. The story begins with an act of turning away and it ends with a return or a turning back. In this way, confession is twice connected to freedom. First, the act confessed is a free act of betrayal. Absent that freedom, the act would be only a mistake or an accident, not a sin. We might regret it, but we would not feel the same need to take responsibility for it. Second, the confession itself amounts to a new assertion of freedom. Confessing, we imagine the possibility of remaking ourselves. Implicit in the confession is belief in the possibility of a new beginning. The narrative of confession is the appearance of freedom before an omnipotent God.

That we must confess *to* someone suggests that freedom is something that we do together. If no one is listening, there can be no confession. Odd as it may sound, confession insists on dialogue—reciprocal recognition—even within an extreme asymmetry of power. This is why disregard, even more than disagreement, can feel like a denial of freedom. Confession may ask for forgiveness, but its deeper point is recognition. Truly to forgive is to engage with a free agent. To accept the sinner is not to make excuses for his or her actions. Forgiveness is closer to mercy than to justice, although forgiveness may go hand-in-hand with justice. There is some truth in the saying, "Forgive the sinner, not the sin." When confession fails to find forgiveness, we are stuck in an in-between zone. That is exactly where my parents ended: they saw each other, but they could not embrace each other. They struggled with the burden of the past without seeing any way forward.

Confession, then, is a self-presentation that is also a demand that one subject makes upon another. It insists on recognition, while exposing our vulnerability to others. In our modern world, confession is the point at which freedom and love confront each other; the only confessions that matter are those to whom we love. Confessing, we put that love at risk, for the response can be hatred. This is not very different from what the Christian penitent found in his act of confessing to a loving God. Because he was free, he could sin; because he could sin, he needed God's love. Confessing his sin, however, he risked God's hatred. Nothing is ever all that new.

For the believer, sin is the barrier that the free will puts between God and the self. Every sin asserts the power of man to live without God. This is the betrayal that begins with Adam. Confession may look like an effort to subordinate the self to God, but in the end, something is left over: the affirmation of the self in the face of God's will. We confess our injustices, but no one confesses simply for the sake of justice. God is on his own in seeking perfect justice. Every confession combines the acknowledgment of wrong—I did *this*—with the affirmation of freedom—*I* did this. This is the paradox of confession. When my adolescent children confessed their misdeeds, they were doing a lot more than registering their injustices. Asking my forgiveness, they were telling me about their independence. Confessing, they were forcing me to see who they were. They were celebrating their own lives; they were demanding recognition. "I am here," they were saying. "Yes, I did this. You can punish me, but you cannot make me other than I am." They needed to know—and to know from me—that freedom need not be a barrier to love.

Confession might once have been, but it is no longer, a ritual; it is not magic, but a moral drama. In the past, confession might have been forced. It might even have been forced by torture. Not so today, when freedom is our lodestar. Unless we confess freely, the confession will fail. Confessing, we freely put the self before God—or, in my mother's case, before my father. As a drama of freedom, we cannot know what the response will be. Just as my father put his questions to the rabbi, my mother put her question to my father. Both failed the test. My father left the temple, but my mother stayed with my father.

My mother's betrayal was above all a free act. This she freely did. It may have been wrong, but it was not a mistake or an accident. So, too, was her confession a free act. Unlike her ordinary talk, here she paused. She looked at the past and the future. Confessing, she took responsibility for her past and she affirmed her belief in a new beginning. This was no mere rushing forward. She staked their world on her freedom and his love. She lost this wager.

My mother's confession may have represented poor judgment, but it stuck to the narrative line. Freedom was twice at issue: in the betrayal and again in the confession. Confessing, she told of her free act. It was only a short step from setting forth the deed, to affirming the deed. "This is what I did. I did it freely; it is my mark upon the world." Confessing to my father, she was not giving up her freedom, but claiming it. Claim may be too strong a word. Just as one cannot claim grace from God, one cannot claim recognition from one's partner. She put the case. After her confession, it was up to him to decide what to do.

The connection of love to recognition is already present in the oldest story we have of the free act. Eve freely chooses sin because she would be like God. She may have been made in the image of God, but still she would refashion herself as even more "godlike." She would have the same knowledge of good and evil as God. How can we not be proud of our freedom? When Eve tells Adam that she has sinned, he follows her out of love. He had lived without her and could not endure the loneliness. He does not have the power to undo the sin; he has only power to accept her, to affirm that she is an inseparable part of his world. He must love the free person, even as she is the source of unending pain.

God's answer to their sin is to exile them from the garden, but Adam's answer to Eve is love. Love is the redemptive act of grace that can respond to our experience of freedom as a fear of failure. Without love, we would be unbearably lonely in our freedom. Love is beyond justice; it must be, for our sin is original, meaning it is unavoidable. When my mother confessed to my father, he could have responded as Adam did with love or as God did with exile. In fact, he could not decide. Everything in him urged exile—to drive her out—but he was as bound to her as Adam was to Eve.

Adam and Eve learn one sure thing from their free act: that they will die. They never make it to the tree of life. Every free act carries within it an image of death, for every free act happens only once. Animals are without freedom because they live without the knowledge of their death. They tell no stories about themselves that begin at birth and end with death. Their behavior repeats itself. Presented the same circumstances, they will do the same thing. People act in history; they act for reasons, not on causes. Circumstances do not repeat for a subject with memory and hope. Each of us knows that our time is limited, that we have a singular past and only one future. The reasons for our actions are set in the singular narrative that is a life.

We each die alone, and thinking about that death is the beginning of that loneliness. A free person needs morality to guide choice—this is a matter of justice. But more than morality, the free person needs love, for justice alone has no power over death. This is the deep lesson of Adam and Eve. Acting justly will not cure our loneliness. Confession plots the way from justice to love. My mother had found her way to the very truth of freedom.

Take God out of the picture I have described. Now, you have my parents. No God, no biblical text, no ritual, not even a temple with a friendly rabbi. How do the old confront their approaching deaths, when the ordinary activities of daily life no longer divert their attention? For my mother, those ordinary diversions had been her endless conversations. Always rushing forward, she saw finally what it was toward which she was moving: death. "Talk" or "die" were no longer the options. It was "talk" *and* "die." My mother wanted from her confession what people have always wanted: to be caught up in the enduring meaning of the universe, to be told that she was not alone and that her life was bound to a larger order. That she was indeed loved.

This is how I think of my mother's strange turn to confession at age seventy-five. She sought grace on a human scale. But from my father of all people? Kindness is not a word that springs to mind when I think of him. Lack of patience does; so does intolerance. I do not remember him ever expressing sympathy for someone's troubles or pains. His general attitude toward such unpleasantness was to turn away. What could she have been thinking? Since my mother often did not think much at all before she talked, it would be easy to suspect that her turn to confession was just an unfortunate turn of direction. That suspicion would be wrong. She thought hard about this. It is just not clear that she understood her situation, for my father was not going to embrace the sinner.

My father knew how to blame but not how to forgive. He never forgave anyone. He never forgave my mother right up to the moment of her death. If to forgive is divine, then my father's militant atheism eliminated any capacity for forgiveness. An entirely secular person, he believed in justice, not forgiveness. But confession is above all a claim on love. My mother's confession put my father to the test. Could he love the sinner? Could he love my mother, all of her—even that part that betrayed him? She wanted to know this, not because she was curious. She wanted to know it in the biblical sense: to know it in her flesh. She wanted to be free and to be loved.

The religious traditions help me to understand my parents, but these traditions were not part of my parents' ordinary world. Yet both of them were feeling their way among these great themes of justice and recognition, of sin and love. Confession is not an act that anyone—secular, Jewish, or Christian—can take up in our society without feeling that she is walking on sacred ground or at least stumbling around among the very foundations of Western practices and beliefs. Without recognizing at least this much, it is simply not possible to come to terms with my mother's confession or my father's response. These most irreligious people were acting out the terms of a Western religious practice of sin, confession, and grace—all of which claimed them despite themselves. Not to see this would strip their story of its meaning; it would deny the truth that they reached only with great pain.

My mother betrayed my father; she confessed. I am sure that she thought that he had often betrayed her. His betrayals were not sexual, but his injustices were many. One could start with the objects flying about the room in his blind rages. Then, there was the disregard of her interests in stability, friendship, and community. She had forgiven his trespasses over the years. She did so out of love. She started down this path of confession to my father thinking that it would make things right between them. She discovered—they both discovered—the surprising character of power that is always present in the act of confession.

Her act of betrayal had come to seem the moment of freedom that defined who she was. She would not let go of it. She insisted on recognition. He could not forgive; he would blot her out rather than recognize her. My mother's confession started a war. By the end, her confession was as much about twisting the knife as seeking peace. Wars end not with forgiveness but with defeat. Neither of my parents, however, had enough power to defeat the other. They could only fight to the end.

What was it she had so desperately to confess? Sex. What else could it have been? I did not know the man, and fortunately, he was long dead. I say fortunately, because if he were not, I am quite sure my father would have thought endlessly about how he needed to kill him. He would have thought he needed to wipe out every trace of memory of the act. Not that he would have done it. He might call everyone an idiot, but he had no taste for personal confrontation. His violence ran toward smashing things, not hitting people. Failure to act in this case, however, would have appeared to him as cowardice, and he already had enough to rage over without adding this particular element of self-hatred.

The hidden secret of my mother's life, we all learned, was an affair that she had had some thirty years earlier. Thirty years may sound like a long time, but in these matters, it is no time at all. The imagination is not bound to the calendar. The memory of the body can be instantaneous. A smell, a glimpse, a sound can take us back immediately to the distant past. This is why torture victims can get no peace. The same is true of lovers. All of those advertisements that appear on the computer, promising to locate your high school classmates, are about love lost but still remembered. Those companies do all right, but not because members of the football team are rediscovering each other. It is not the first drink but the first touch that haunts memory. These things can be neither shared nor expelled from memory.

For most people, these memories are only pleasant—or not-so-pleasant—daydreams. They do not intrude deeply into the normal routines and responsibilities of our lives. Thirty years after the fact, this affair moved from the periphery to the center of my mother's memories. When she thought about herself, this is what she saw: not the routine of family, but her secret lover. My mother, who always rushed into the future, found herself dwelling in the past. This was not because she was overwhelmed by guilt, but because she was remembering the exceptional.

The exception is always more powerful than the routine, for it sets the limits of our lives. For veterans, it is often their wartime experience, brief as it might have been, that leaves the most enduring memory. The rest of us share something of this when we consider the impact of 9/11. This, we cannot forget. The exceptional need not be destructive: I remember the moment of the birth of each of my children; I remember the first time I saw Catherine. And, I remember when I first heard my mother's confession.

The memory of the act was, for my mother, more powerful and more demanding than the thought of its injustice. If it were only the wrong that was bothering her, she would not have been led to confession. We all have a personal statute of limitations that covers our injustices. Surely, my mother could have measured her wrongs against my father's, and decided they were even. Identity, not justice, was at issue. The idea gave her strength. "I have lived. I have been my own person. I broke all the rules and expectations. I acted for myself." She was proud of her free act. It came to seem her most authentic moment.

The war that opened up between my parents was over who would claim the credit for the storyline that was their life together. The battle was so vicious because they were fighting about a myth: how to tell the story of their lives. Whole societies tear themselves apart over competing myths: Was Jesus the Messiah or a wayward Jew? The same impulses can drive the smaller battles within a family. We need to know who we are, and for my parents that question opened up in a terrifying way when my mother hit seventy-five.

Neither of my parents had been in the habit of reflecting on the past. They avoided public displays of memory. There was no sense in their house that there had ever been a past. There were no photographs of their children or grandchildren hanging on the walls. No pictures of their parents, let alone grandparents. No framed awards; no mementoes of family outings. Nothing of my parents' past life together: no wedding photos, no vacation memorabilia, no shots of old homes or old celebrations. Instead, there were some starkly abstract paintings and some paintings of tranquil scenes—mostly maritime. There were books, but no photo albums. Once, when I was young, I had found an old shoebox full of photos my parents had taken before my birth, including even pictures from the War. That box had long ago disappeared.

Their life seemed always in the present. They liked to read magazines; they never kept back issues. If there was one object of veneration in the house, it was the daily *New York Times*. A life in the present was one way to respond to the painful history of the twentieth century. So it seemed to me. My mother's childhood, after all, was a story of dawning awareness of a genocidal anti-Semitism, then the escape from Hitler, and finally arrival in New York. My father's childhood matched my mother's in pain, if not in political fear. His father had died when he was still a toddler, transforming their well-off household into one of hopeless poverty. He grew up in the Great Depression. Relatives had supported him and his mother, until the War offered him a way out. With such childhoods, it was not surprising that they did not dwell on the past.

They were carried along on the familiar post-war story of progress. Carried quite literally from urban poverty and wartime violence to life in the suburbs. Both made the transition via a public university. They arrived in suburbia educated and with a steady income. Just the conditions to start a family, which they did. Suburban living would be fine compared to what they had been through. Both of my grandfathers had been butchers, but my parents were professionals. This is what America meant in the boom of the 1950s. Life would be forward movement. Children growing up, houses getting bigger, savings accruing interest. No looking back: not to the Depression, not to the War, not ever. That suited them just fine. They saw nothing to celebrate in that past; nothing to pass on.

By the time of their retirement, all of this seemed to have more or less played out according to the plan, despite the unsettled career choices of my father. First, he had been a chemist; then a lawyer. Finally, he settled into running a small business—a marina on the upper reaches of the Chesapeake. By sixty-five, he had cashed out. He was done with work, which he had never enjoyed very much. Dealing with people had never been his strength. He liked to putter: small jobs around the house were what he liked best. On retirement, he could look back satisfied: his diverse occupations had successfully brought his children to adulthood and him to security.

My parents had enough money to live out their lives in a comfortable condominium, first in Wilmington, Delaware, and then in Connecticut. They wintered in Florida. My mother had neighbors with whom she enjoyed talking. My father was busy enough reading the *Times* and repairing whatever he could find to fix. To my surprise, he tried out several art classes at the local community college—the retirement equivalent of the always-unsettled character of his career choices. Both parents were fine, I thought. Apart from health issues, I did not have to worry about them.

They were now grandparents and mostly enjoyed that role. They were happy to do their duty, if we asked them to stay with the kids for a few days while we went away. They, no less than the kids, however, would be counting the days until we got back. I never thought about it. Now, I think it hard to be an enthusiastic grandparent without the sentimentality that comes from remembrance. They did not regale our children with stories about what it was like when their father was little. They had no photo albums to pull out. They did not have the endless patience required to delight in the self-absorption of small children. They were fine, but their lives always seemed elsewhere. Most of all, they had each other. They were completely entwined in each other's life. They did not have separate pursuits or their own friends.

It was easy to look at them and see escapees from the earlier part of the century. They would not look back because there was only violence, poverty, and pain in their childhoods. There was death as well. This was something about which we never talked. But I knew that most of my mother's large family did not survive the Holocaust. Indeed, I bear the name of one of them. As for my father, he was a member of that generation of veterans who never spoke a word of their experience of battle. How could he not carry with him images of the dead and dying on the beaches and in the forests of Europe? With such memories, it made perfect sense that my parents never dwelled on the past. They had each other. They lived life mostly on the surface, neither remembering the past nor planning ahead. Next winter in Florida was the outer measure of their plans.

In thinking that the pattern of their lives had been shaped by the Depression and the War, I was only partly right. The latter part of the twenieth century, I thought, was mine, not theirs. What I did not realize then was that they, too, were products of the 1960s. I had thought them old by the time the sixties arrived, but they were considerably younger than I am now. I thought the sixties had been about youth, meaning my generation. But we had no life that the sixties might challenge. We were unformed. We thought that we were rebelling against our parents, but what generation has not thought that? There was no real revolution in our lives because there was not yet enough of a life to revolt against. Look at us now. We mostly live the same sort of lives as our parents. We are teachers, doctors, lawyers, and businessmen. We live in the same houses in suburbia and send our children to the same colleges and universities. So much for the revolution.

Not so my parents' experience of the sixties. Revolution meant something for them beyond putting up some posters and smoking a little pot. Their post-war world of suburban stability came to seem entirely false—a charade of manners. In their own ways, each of them lit a fuse that would destroy the other. It was just that in my mother's case it was a very long fuse and it was not until she was seventy-five that the explosion finally arrived.

I was a teenager in those years of counterculture, and mostly I remember my parents' resistance to my behavior. My hair was too long, my music too loud, my actions too irresponsible. As with everything else, however, they were not very deeply invested in this resistance. Nothing much ever came of it. I went my own way and they just stopped nagging after a little while. I thought I had won, but in truth, they just gave up the game. They let me go, because they, too, were going their own way. I had no idea that they had already abandoned our suburban life. The family fell apart for lack of care. Both of my parents were looking elsewhere.

One memory sticks out: my first day of college in 1969. I loaded some clothes and a lot of books into a big, green, army-surplus duffel bag and then flew standby from New Jersey to Chicago. I took public transportation from the airport to the city. I dragged the heavy bag the last mile up the street to my new dorm, arriving physically exhausted. What is striking now as I recall the event is the complete absence of my parents. I was seventeen; I was on my own. As a parent now, I find this hard to fathom. When my children started college, there were weeks of preparation, drives across the country, rental of hotel rooms, tours of the campus, help with registration, trips to the mall to buy room furnishings, meetings with the roommate's family, and, finally, tearful goodbyes. All of this was followed by multiple phone calls every day, discussing every possible concern. "What is a demand curve? Should I take kickboxing? How do I make brownies? I don't like my roommate's music." It never ends. With my parents, it never began. Not once did they visit me in college. They would have been puzzled by the very suggestion. What would they do, were they to come?

The times were different, Catherine tells me. That is certainly true, but how so? What can be so different about love? We are a part of each other's lives or we are not. I try not to intrude too deeply in my children's lives, but not for one moment do I let them think that I do not care deeply about all that they do, all that they feel, and all that they believe. There is never any doubt in their minds that I am ready to do anything for them. Fortunately, my children do not test the far end of this proposition very often.

I am sure the times were different, but that does not mean that there can be love without care. Not care in the abstract, but the care in which we are a part of each other's lives. No, the truth is harder. It was the sixties, and everyone was worrying too much about themselves to invest very much in anyone else. Our family was not pathological. It was noteworthy for its normalcy. What that meant was it was not the center of anybody's life. We all went our own ways. Love has to be earned. It is not a fallback position. This family never earned much love. Serviceable, but not loving. It is not written anywhere that family must be the center of your life. The sixties were about alternative lifestyles. Our family did not fall apart; it just never built up much speed. To this day, I rarely see my brother and sister. We did not bond in childhood, and we have not in later life. We get along, but we have all built our own lives.

So there I was, with that heavy duffel bag. I was not alienated; I was excited by the future opening up as I walked down the street. I never asked them for help. They never offered. I was busy stopping the war in Vietnam, or watching new French movies, or taking up the practice of Zen Buddhism. It never occurred to me that they did not try to stop any of this because they were wondering whether they should be doing the same thing. Indeed, they were doing the same things.

These things, however, looked entirely different to them. What seemed natural to me was entirely revolutionary to them. The sixties challenged everything about their lives. None of this registered with me, but now I see it as the great turning point in their lives. It seemed entirely reasonable to me that when my father turned fifty, he announced that he had quit his well-paying corporate job. "Good move," I thought. No more of that for him; he would buy a marina. Goodbye to the suburbs, to commuting, to suits and business trips. He would spend the rest of his life puttering around boats. It hardly caused a ripple in my life. I even spent a few months, immediately after college graduation, giving him a hand. During the day, we would work on boats. At night, I would study classical Greek at the kitchen table, while he read *The New Yorker* in the living room. That was as close as we ever got.

To my mother, this move from a suburban life did not seem reasonable at all. Her revolution had not yet arrived. She was happy with her career, her friends, and the endless occasions for talk in suburban life. She could not use the children as an excuse to stay—the last of us had gone off to college. Nor could she imagine staying without him. She was certainly not prepared to be single. It would be too lonely. To whom would she talk? There was not yet any place in suburbia for the divorcee. Everyone she knew was part of a couple. An empty apartment would be nothing but silence. This was simply unthinkable.

I do not think my mother plotted revenge when my father moved her to the marina in rural Maryland. She just found herself completely unsettled. Her life was not working out. This was not like a corporate transfer to a new state where the individuals change but the roles stay the same. It was as if her husband announced that they were joining a commune. Indeed, there was not much difference between that and the goodbye to suburbia that my father planned. Maybe a commune would have been better for my mother since there would have been plenty of people around. A marina in the middle of nowhere. What was she supposed to do? She was not about to paint boat bottoms. There were no other women around. To whom exactly was she going to talk?

This was certainly not what she had planned. My father did not consult with her on the decision. There was, in his view, nothing to talk about. His corporate life was an intolerable falsehood. If his life was a lie, the answer was not discussion but decision. He did not need therapy; he needed a complete change. The sixties had taught him that we are each responsible for making our own lives. He and I were on the same page on this point. Authenticity was our guiding star. Other people would have to join us—or stick with us—on our own terms. Of course, I was twenty while he was fifty. Authenticity had been the last thing on my mother's mind when my father declared his new life. But how to respond?

She joined the revolution. My father might give up suits for overalls. She would give up monogamy. Which was the stronger lesson of the sixties: the freedom to reinvent oneself or free sex? These two messages were so closely tied together that the pill could become the symbol of the entire era. My father would wear work clothes and work with his hands—honest labor. My mother would wear nothing at all—honest sex. Each thought living in the truth meant living a simpler life with simpler satisfactions. No more false roles, only authenticity. Her idea of authenticity, however, was not something she could share with him. In truth, his idea of authenticity was not really something he shared with her. I do not remember ever seeing her out on the docks or comfortable in a boat.

If he could abandon his suburban life, what exactly could be wrong with her having an affair? The only value that truly mattered was the free creation of one's self. One had to experiment in life: work, drugs, sex. Life was to be experienced. They both had come to the belief that ordinary forms and expectations were simply barriers to realizing deeper truths. The real danger was not in change, but in holding back and failing to live life fully. I wondered what kinds of drugs they had experimented with.

My mother was not going to find herself tending boats, but she was nevertheless going to find herself. The need to act freely was the lesson she had learned from my father. Actually, it was the lesson that was being proclaimed everywhere around her. My father's act of free abandon gave her the occasion, and perhaps even the courage, to express her own freedom. In the 1960s, we were all lugging our own duffle bags through life, and it was up to each of us to make a life that was genuine and true. Authenticity was the goal. Commitment looked uncomfortably like failure in an age in which anything was possible.

Both of my parents, in their own ways, abandoned suburban life, including its ideal of the family. His was an explicit revolution; hers was a secret revolution. People could joke about his new lifestyle. He had gone from corporate attorney to "Capt'n Sam." I suspect that she told plenty of jokes about her husband's revolutionary change of life. She told them, however, while lying in someone else's bed. Who was more authentic: My father in his revolt against middle-class professional values or my mother in her revolt against middle-class sexual mores? Revolution has a funny way of turning into betrayal. Each was living out the meaning of freedom in the sixties. They were just not doing it together. Each was betraying the other, for neither was acting with care for the other.

Had their life been a comedy, each would have recognized the need of the other to revolt against their common, suburban lifestyle. They would, however, have discovered that the deeper truth was their own relationship. They would, in other words, have been brought back together in the end, wiser for what they had learned about themselves and about each other. Their new roles as Capt'n Sam and secret lover would have come to seem mistaken. The promise of those roles had been only an illusion of authenticity. Real life is closer to home; it is in family and ordinary pursuits. They would have made this renewed life together.

Comedy always ends in reconciliation and then enduring happiness. My mother, at seventy-five, wanted her life story to end as romantic comedy. She had no idea that tragedy was sitting out there as an alternative plotline, for she never read tragedy.

The first step, my mother thought, was to confess to her sexual transgression of thirty years earlier. Heartfelt confession might produce some tears. Then would come the all-night discussions as they went over their past life together. She would tell him how upset she had been by his decision to abandon their suburban home. She would say that she had been hurt and confused, that she had needed support, that, in fact, the affair had been a good thing because it had led her to see that really she did want to stay with him. She had, after all, chosen him; she had not left. The whole affair was her path of self-discovery, just as his turn to the marina had been his similar path. Then, of course, there were all those years that they had had together since the affair. Surely, those years were what counted now. They would come through this together and live out their final years in the well-earned peace of old age. She saw them walking on the beach holding hands as they recognized how fortunate they really had been. Just think of Hitler and how bad it could have been. The sixties would appear as a mere aberration, a detour, in a longer life story that began in a small town in Germany and ended on a Florida beach. Theirs was an enduring love.

I am sure that she played this script out in her head; she discussed it with her therapist. Since nothing she had ever said had caused a deep reaction, she had no reason to think that turning her talk in this direction would bring disaster. She was wholly unprepared when her effort to write this script entirely failed. Their life turned into nothing but tragedy. In college, I learned that comedy and tragedy are ultimately the same thing. From the outside, there was something comic about this endless war between two old people over something that may never have happened. From the inside, there was nothing funny about it at all.

She confessed and my father had to decide: comedy or tragedy, love or hatred? He was not prepared to play the role of comic character in her drama. He had already completed his own script. That script too was comedy—people never write tragedies for themselves. In his drama, however, he had successfully gone from corporate lawyer to Capt'n Sam. His comedy was not a romance. In fact, my mother barely appeared in his script, despite the well-hidden fact that the success of his marina depended more on her continued income than on his puttering. The script was about his successful revolt against the corporate world, about finding his authentic self among the boats and the characters in a small town along the water's edge. His script was a character study of himself; its theme was the possibility of authenticity even in modern America. My mother's role in his script was only to be there to testify to his success.

In his script, he proved that one really could give it all up. He had considerable pride in his iconoclasm. He had successfully traded business suits for overalls. He was the object, he thought, of considerable admiration among all those poor suckers who never made it out of the office. He had done that of which they had only dreamed. They might have more money, but he had enough. He had lived his own life and survived to tell the tale. For the rest of his life, he expected to hear admiring reviews from friends and acquaintances. He had an endless store of tales to tell of life at the marina, all of which had a single theme: once you become your own man, there is nothing that anyone can do to you.

My mother's confession tore up his script. There was indeed something that someone could do to you: your wife could murder you. She could tell you that your entire life had been a lie. Like Oedipus fleeing his father only to kill him, my father had sought freedom only to live a lie. My mother offered him a new role: cuckold. He was not going to play that role. If she wanted romantic comedy, he would give her only tragedy. No long, heart-felt conversations deep into the night. No walks on the beach. There would be only rage, endless roaring rage that knew no limits.

If he had not been approaching old age, I would have feared physical violence. Actually, I did fear violence at times. But really he had no need to strike her, for he well understood the methods of psychological torture. He had been a medic in the War, but his true skills lay elsewhere: in destroying, not saving, lives. My mother had not one moment of peace, no rest at all, until the moment of her death. Not even her final struggle with cancer offered a respite from my father's rage. He filled the space of their mutual life with his outsized anger. When he was not screaming, belittling, bullying, and demeaning, he was sulking and getting ready to attack again. There was nothing she could do that was right because there was nothing she could do to make it right.

His fury knew no bounds. He knew no quiet. He gave up sleep. He gave up everything. He lived for one purpose: to hound her to the end of her days. When he was not raging against her, he was in tears over what she had done to him. He needed to make sure that not for one moment would she think that her affair had been a moment of authenticity. All that it was and ever could be was betrayal. It was a crime for which he would extract every possible ounce of suffering. King Lear proclaims to Cordelia, when he feels his love betrayed, "out of my sight." That, my father thought, would have been too good for my mother. He had no intention of leaving her or letting her out of his sight. In fact, he clung to her obsessively. His objective was torture, not banishment. She was to know that she was nothing and that he was everything.

My father's rage was driven by his deep sense of betrayal. My mother's confession had pierced some boundary of the imagination that was just irreparable. She had destroyed him. Each time he imagined her betrayal, he felt it as his own murder. "Where am I?" he kept crying to himself. The answer he could not fathom was the one he kept having forced upon him: "I am not."

They were now locked in a battle and each had found the tools to destroy the other. Her endlessly repeated confession was a mortal blow each time he heard it. That she was repeating it to everyone was a way of making him suffer a thousand deaths. By confessing to others, she was preempting his effort to tell the world of her sin. His screaming rage was meant to destroy her again and again. He would loosen his rage against her for others to see. He would abuse her in public. When others tried to defend her, he would turn on them. They quickly lost all of their friends. They were like two wounded animals who could not be pulled apart. I could not bear to be near them, but neither could I stay away.

Only the uninitiated would see in their war her weakness and his strength. He was indeed louder and more violent. He would throw things and say the most disgusting things. He would call her a slut. She was a bimbo fucking another man. She had destroyed her family and betrayed her children. Always she was the "fucking whore." But she would come back at him with "I was upset and lonely" or "I needed support and you were not there." In his ears, this was all a way of saying "yes, I fucked him and I did it to you because you deserved no less. You were nothing to me." She was no less skilled at making him suffer than he was at making her suffer. She knew how to say that which he could not bear to hear, and she would not be silent. Talk or die.

He may have yelled louder, but her endless confessions inflicted just as much pain. More, I suspect. He could not live with this confession ringing in his ears. He always seemed more desperate than she did. Of course, her position gathered considerably more sympathy from others. Not just because of the outrage his language would cause, but because no one really had much sympathy for his claim to have suffered an unbearable wound. No one could take too seriously that an old man would charge murder for an act of sexual transgression some thirty years past. Hadn't he heard of the sexual revolution? But his pain was real and there was nothing that could be done to relieve it.

Could my mother really have so misjudged the man she had spent her life with that she believed her confession could bring forth forgiveness and recognition? Did she really imagine that they would walk down the beach together, reminiscing about their past? Always she would come back to the same romantic image of old age as reconciliation and peace. This was what she needed now. She needed him to embrace her as she imagined herself. At this moment, she thought of herself not as the refugee from Germany and not as the post-War suburban homemaker. The authentic moment in her life was the exceptional moment; it was the free act of transgression. The exceptional stands out in memory.

My mother did err—or maybe she just forgot—in her repeated explanations of what had been at stake thirty years earlier. When she said that she had been unhappy and needed support in a difficult time, I heard what memory made of the event, long after the excitement of the affair was gone. Memory makes excuses. Back then, she was not looking for excuses. The issue had been revolution and freedom, no less for her than for him. Her affair was a celebration of life, not a desperate search for solace. Free love had been a political and personal statement. It was not a flight from life but a claim for authenticity. It was this lingering sense of authenticity that drove her to confession. She had no interest in atoning for her sin. She wanted recognition for the act that remained uniquely hers.

Why did my mother, who managed to keep silent about this but nothing else for thirty years, take a new course at seventy-five? Why this need to confess now? It was as if two distinct pathways in her mind had crossed. On the one hand, there was the ceaseless talk. On the other, there was the ceaseless brooding over that which was never spoken. Suddenly, that which she could never say was all that she could say.

I suspect that the immediate source of my mother's plan to confess to my father was some very bad therapeutic advice. Betrayal and sin are not categories that come easily to the mind of the modern therapist. Honesty, strength, equality, authenticity, and self-determination are the right categories. The point of therapy would have been to help my mother gain strength as an individual. She was to be honest with herself, make her own decisions, and then insist that those who deal with her recognize her for who she is. Whatever she had done, she had done for reasons. Honestly confronting those reasons would be the path to happiness. It is a principle of modern therapy that nothing is unforgivable. If everything is forgivable, then everything can be spoken. Truth is the beginning and end of the process. Everything is to be put out in the open. For Freud, even oedipal longings are to be confessed. To the therapist, the claim that some things might be unbearable is itself a sign of pathology, of a need for more therapy.

My mother, I am sure, explained to the therapist all the reasons for her affair: she had been unhappy, she had not wanted to move from suburbia, her children had all left home, and she had become uncertain about her relationship to my father. The normal stuff of the therapeutic encounter. The therapist probably told her that if acknowledging the affair would help her to come to terms with her own life, my father would have to live with the knowledge. Perhaps she suggested that what they really needed was couples therapy. A trained counselor could help them to talk through all of this so that they could go on with their lives without the burden of a hidden and unresolved past. Valuable relationships must, after all, be built on honesty. This, I imagine, was the tenor of the therapist's advice.

I doubt it would have crossed the therapist's mind that my father's reaction would be murderous. He was, after all, approaching eighty. Could it occur to the therapist that he would have murdered her as well, if he had had the strength? I am sure he came to imagine her death a thousand times. Her sin was that she knew, yet she did not condemn. She actually took my mother's side, instead of turning her out. In my father's world, this was idolatry. Idolatry is a capital offense.

If the therapist thought of the possibility of violence at all, she imagined calling the police and obtaining a restraining order. She must have had a standard protocol to follow in such cases. The law—police and family court—would be there to help realize a modern solution to my mother's problem. The solution might be for her to leave him, if he could not live with the truth. As soon as my mother walked into that office, the question of whether to stay or to leave my father was an issue. It had to be, because she came in alone. The one thing she did for sure when she entered was to leave him outside. In her conversation with the therapist, she had already left him once. What she would do when she went back out the door was an open question. Should she go home or should she go to her sister's?

This is why my father hated my mother's trips to the therapist. He felt the exclusion of the closing door. He knew that they were talking about him and what to do about him. He felt that talk not just as an abandonment, but also as a violation. He had not invited the therapist into his life. He did not think that he was accountable to her, even as he knew that there was much in his life for which he could be held to account. My parents had created a world together, but who exactly was to control the borders of that world? Who would decide to allow entry of the stranger? My father always wanted to deny entry. My mother was always bringing in guests. The therapist was the uninvited guest whom my father could not exclude.

There is not all that much difference between therapy and an affair. They ran together in my father's mind: each involved an uninvited guest in his life. Both are free acts of choosing to share an intimacy with another. Each is a turning away and a turning toward. This is exactly what Freud's theory of transference is all about. For the duration of the therapy, the psychoanalyst stands in for the object of love. My father heard the "not you" in these therapeutic encounters. He felt the endless need to play the voyeur—first to the conversation with the therapist and then to the affair with the lover. He thought of both the therapist and the lover as occupying his place. He could get neither out of his mind.

There is a reason that a secular culture that grew up in the shadow of the religious confession would have a particular interest in the "talking cure." The therapist holds out the same promise as the priest: forgiveness and recognition. This is, of course, just what we want from love. Priest, therapist, and lover stand together—or do they stand in competition? Each is assigned the care of the soul. Each makes the same promise of acceptance. Today, we are not sure whether to believe in any of them. Each demands faith in his or her own way. Faith, however, is in short supply. Without faith, priests become social workers, and therapists increasingly turn from the practice of confession to the prescription of medication. Pharmaceuticals cannot fill the place of recognition. At best, they can quiet the demand. Only love still promises the possibility of recognition and freedom.

My mother's medicine cabinet did begin to fill up with prescriptions—a sure sign that she was "getting help." The drugs helped her sleep; they did not answer the basic need. Neither rabbi nor therapist could do that. Only my father could. My mother did not want to think differently about herself. She did not want to come to terms with herself; she wanted my father to come to terms with her. She wanted her confession to restore a world of love. This, however, is an entirely unmodern idea. It is beyond the therapist's power to deliver, and beyond the power of law to protect. It too requires a kind of faith, for there cannot be love without the lover's faith in the beloved. We put ourselves in each other's trust.

At seventy-five, my mother had a romantic idea of the two of them looking back over their entire lives together and embracing it all as their story. Nothing would be unspoken; nothing kept secret. She learned at therapy that speaking honestly can make you stronger. She became convinced that she could transfer the talk of the therapist's office to talk with my father. If the therapist could hear the truth and assure her that all was fine, then why not my father? Betrayal, however, is not explained away as self-discovery. My mother was entering a world of extremes and no therapist was going to be able to help her. There was no prescription adequate to this pain; there were no rituals of forgiveness or redemption in my father's world. She was moving from a modern world of therapeutic intervention to a biblical world of righteous vengeance. Wanting love, she got war.

I had no more insight than anyone else did when I first heard my mother's confession. "Of all things," I thought. Her life had spanned most of the twentieth century. She must have had memories of *Krystallnacht*, of Franklin Roosevelt, of wartime New York, of Hiroshima, of the Cuban Missile Crisis, even of the Beatles' arrival in New York. If she insisted now on bringing up the past, could she not speak of the great events that she had witnessed? The old owe to the young the passing on of such memories. She should be telling my children about what life was like before the computer and the smartphone. Instead, she wanted to talk about sex. Old sex at that. Who cares? This was not a conversation for my children. It was not a conversation for her children. I certainly had no desire to hear any of this. I, however, had little choice. The phone rang and, through her desperate crying and my father's hysterical screaming, I heard her say, "I told him." I said, "We will be right there."

By the time Catherine and I arrived at their condominium, the pattern had already been established that would last the rest of my mother's life. Both my parents were in a kind of shock. She was chattering and cowering. He was cycling between hysterical crying and raging. He grasped me as I came in. Before this, we never touched. Not at least in my memory. Of course, before this I had never seen my father in tears. Before this, he had not really appeared old. Between morning and afternoon, he had literally become an old man: broken, overwhelmed, and suddenly dependent. He grasped me as if he were about to collapse. His physical strength had drained away. What had happened to him seemed worse than experiencing the death of a loved one. I suppose for him it was a witnessing of his own death.

Through the hysteria that greeted us, he said something that I found unfathomable in its brutality: "I'm too old to find someone to fuck."

Revenge, not forgiveness, was on his mind. Forgiveness would never be on his mind. Wanting revenge desperately, he felt overwhelmed by defeat. If only he had learned earlier, he was saying, he could have responded in kind. She struck at him twice. First, in the affair itself; second, in waiting to tell him until it was too late for him to act. He wanted sevenfold vengeance like that threatened by God to protect Cain. To no avail, for he was too old. If she did not yet have the last word, she had already had the last act. Years before, my father had told me that "in life there are only two kinds of people, the fuckers and the fuckees." I thought this odd advice in a conversation about my interest in an academic career. Now I saw its meaning. At this moment, he was, and thought he would remain forever, the fuckee.

My mother had begun her confession bravely, following a set script. She had rehearsed it not just with the therapist, but many, many times in her own mind. She would tell him that there was something she felt she had to share with him. Something had been weighing on her mind for years. She was ready with her explanations. He needed to understand the reasons behind her actions. She would review all the turmoil in their lives back then. He had to see that her reaction to those changes in their lives had been entirely reasonable. She had gone to another man only to find the support that my father had failed to offer. Surely, he could remember how distant he had been from her in those years. She would tell him that she was neither judging, nor blaming. All of this had been long ago and she understood now that he too had had many things that he needed to work out. She had been no different. The important thing was that they had weathered all the ups and downs and had remained together. In the ripeness of age, it was time for truth.

She would not present it as if she were asking his forgiveness; rather, she was sharing something important to both of them. It was not justice that brought her forward now, but the need for each of them to embrace the other fully at the end of life. It was easiest to talk about it as being truthful. They both would be better off, she planned to say, if they recognized the truth of their long relationship—both the good and the bad. Even late in life, a relationship must be built on honesty. To find the strength to be honest was the reason she had gone to therapy. Maybe she would even suggest that he too could see a therapist to help him confront his own difficult truths.

My father did not let her get beyond the first sentence. Her carefully prepared speech was never delivered. Not, in any case, in one piece. There was no patient waiting, while she had her say. The act was all. After he heard that, he stopped listening and started raging. There are some truths we do not care to know. Some we cannot bear to know. First and foremost among these is that of sexual betrayal. There is no neutral position from which one recognizes one's wife in bed with another man. To hear this report is not like learning of an unfortunate physical condition. Adultery is not an accident or an illness. It is more like a gunshot. It hits the body with the force of a bullet. When we arrived, my father was bleeding. My mother was aching with regret for what she had done. It was already clear that her romantic image was not to be—not ever. An entire world had collapsed in an instant and no recovery was possible.

He was not prepared to forgive and, once she told him, he could not forget. Her reasons were entirely beside the point. In his mind, they were not excuses to be considered but more reminders of the fact. He was prepared to do only one thing: rage. He might not be capable of revenge, but he was certainly capable of vengeance. He would destroy her and the whole of their world. They had entered a domain of mutual assured destruction. My mother had launched the first strike. It did not matter why she had done it. It did not matter that it was a mistake, brought on by faulty analysis or bad therapy. She could not call it back. It did its damage. Now we had to wait to see if there would actually be followthrough on the retaliatory threat of world annihilation. We did not have to wait long. Already, the world was being blown to bits by the time Catherine and I arrived.

He was ranting about sexual revenge and lost opportunity. Sex with someone else was obviously not a new thought for him. That was exactly the point. He had thought of it often. There were probably many opportunities over the years: business trips, flirtatious customers, bored spouses. Everyone remembers the hint of a suggestion, an unspoken invitation. However, he had decided against it. With him, I suspect the decision had been based as much on fear as on loyalty, although he might think now that it was more of the latter than the former. He had spent most of his adult life shedding burdens. A lover would have been only another burden. He had little capacity to connect to others. He had no interest in exposing his inner life to another. He wanted no vulnerabilities, which meant for him no responsibilities.

Raging, he was no more interested in exploring the reasons for why he had not acted than he was in considering my mother's excuses. The point was that he could have, but he did not. Without knowing it, he had lost his chance to triumph. That was the injustice he felt—a sort of cosmic disorder. More than anything else, he wanted to be able to meet her claim and up it. He wanted to be able to say, "You slept with one, but I slept with many." He wanted to be able to get back behind those thirty years and show her that his was the power. He wanted to be able to say "you are nothing to me; you have been nothing to me." If their relationship was to be broken to bits, he wanted to be the one who would do the breaking.

His first thoughts were of revenge pure and simple. His reaction was that of an adolescent, seeking to get even. But her reaction, too, was that of an adolescent. I heard from her a flow of excuses as if she were trying to make up to a boyfriend who had gone off to college, leaving her lonely in high school. Or, perhaps more familiar in their case, as if she were writing one of those "Dear John" letters that her generation had written to boyfriends off at the War. There were the bits and pieces of the prepared speech, coming out now in a jumble of banal phrases about loneliness and needing support. He was not listening and she was lost in words that just continued to flow. Her chatter met his declarations.

When I say that their reactions were adolescent, I do not mean to suggest that there was a mature way to handle the situation, which they somehow missed. Adolescence may be when we feel the raw power of sex most acutely. In moments of crisis, we return to the beginning. What is the right way to react to an act of betrayal? We do not register this calmly. We do not go for a walk on the beach to discuss it. The demand for revenge competes with the plea for mercy. No one can know in advance how they will react to such news. Will you turn away or will you embrace the sinner? Will you rage or will you succumb to the despondency of defeat? My father did not turn away and he did not admit defeat. He turned toward my mother with murder in his heart. No one had warned her of this possibility.

No one wants to hear of their parents' sex lives. No one wants these intimate details exploding about. Suddenly, I was hearing things that I wanted to ignore and quickly tried to suppress. Did I hear them trading accusations that they had not slept together in years? Or was it decades? Did I make that up afterwards? Was she saying that he had already stopped sleeping with her before the affair? One does not ask for clarification under these circumstances. I did not even want to trade notes with Catherine after we got home. I did not want to talk to anyone about this. I wanted to avert my eyes from the vision of my naked parents. Having been sullied by the sight, I wanted my own ritual of cleansing. No such ritual was on offer. Like my father, I had neither rabbi nor therapist in my life.

I did not want to know about my mother's affair or my father's sexual frustrations. But neither could I abandon them to themselves. Their relationship was no longer that of a household but that of an open wound. They could not easily go out together because they could not contain their battle. When they did try, he would glare furiously. Eventually, he would erupt in shouts. Then would come her explanations— her confession—to whomever they were with. This only prompted more rage from him. He wanted to make it impossible for the world to hear what she had to say. He would shout her down. Neither would he easily let her go out alone. He feared what she might say to others or maybe he just feared that she would forget for a moment what she had done to him. They remained inseparable.

So they lived in those years, locked in a battle of confession and murderous rage. From him, she would get no forgiveness. From her, he would get no apology. To be with them during this period was like entering a battlefield. When I would show up, a truce would be called for the purpose of carrying out diplomatic negotiations. Each tried to persuade me to join one side of this battle. He would tearfully describe her betrayal. He would mourn his failure to retaliate when he could have. He was no less thinking about sex—and the failure to have sex—than was she. My mother would counter with how miserable she had been with my father. How much she had needed comfort. When I would leave, the truce would end and they would struggle with all the fury that they could muster.

There is no vacation from hell; one does not get to take the afternoon off. It was all fire and brimstone. For neither of them was there to be any peace from this war that they had created for themselves. Professional help was out of the question. He would not think of it for himself and for her to return to therapy would have just provoked more of his fury. I thought of their house as a place that simply radiated pain. I would ache at the very thought of going to see them. I dreaded the ringing of the telephone.

I do not know whether they deserved such misery, but what they did to each other in those years was something I could not have imagined possible. He became a broken man; she became a figure of great pathos, occupying the shadow of his rage. She never took her suffering as a just response to her act of betrayal. Her confession was never about an injustice she had committed. She was making a demand for recognition. When he forced the issue, when he would not turn away from his rage, she fought back in the only way she could. She would keep talking: "I did this." He would never be free of her confession. If his reaction was murderous, her response was no less deadly. They were both skilled executioners.

Their lives took on the quality of fiction—great, tragic fiction. They were bound together in love and hatred. My parents had built a world together. Every bit of that world was now being destroyed. It was as if the memory of their life together was to be removed from history. My role is to save the story. This became the deep puzzle of my life: how can we so hate those we love?

The forces moving them were beyond their ability to understand. My mother found herself on the hard ground of confession, but had come to it with ideas taken from the romantic comedies that she liked to watch. My father believed that he could reason his way through life. Watching him try to reason his way through this was like watching a man possessed by spirits. He would scream, he would cry, he would withdraw, he would rage until he would collapse.

My mother would confess what my father could not bear to hear. That was the unalterable fact. This went on for years. There was no common ground, but neither was there any breaking apart of their embrace. They were quite literally locked into a mutual hatred that occupied all of their time and all of their space. All she could do was offer up her confession; all he could do was rage at that which she insisted that he see. If he could have, he would have blinded himself. But how do you blind yourself to a memory once it has been spoken?

Each became obsessed with the act itself. I think he imagined her in bed with her lover 100 times a day. He could not get the image out of his mind. When he closed his eyes and tried to sleep, this was all that he could see. He stopped sleeping. She too was seized by the image. Endlessly, she would try to explain it. In his rage, he would try to silence her; he would try to scream her into oblivion. Really, however, he needed her to speak. He needed to hear her say "Never mind, I was mistaken. That wasn't me. I had confused my own body for that of another." My mother, however, could only repeat what she had already said: "I was upset. I was lonely. I needed to discover myself. I needed this in order to be sure about you." Each time she set into her renewed confession, she murdered him again. Both of them knew they were torturing each other, but there were no terms of withdrawal available.

Adam stuck with Eve out of love. I suspect, however, that sometimes as he tilled the barren soil and contemplated his own death, he found in himself a raging hatred toward Eve. "Why did she have to do that?" My parents stuck with each other in love and hatred. The difference is not as great as one might think.

Surely, you are thinking, sex is not that big a deal. Many people have affairs and the world does not end. People get back together; they put it behind them. We all make mistakes, but we move on. Did my parents really so confuse sex and love? There must have been something else unsettled, some other problem that this confession brought to the surface. You would be half-right. Right in thinking that it had to be about more than sex, but wrong in thinking that sex was only a sign of some other trouble. Sex is about as elemental as it gets, and my parents had entered a domain in which everything but the most elemental had been destroyed. Sex maintained all of its old power of possession and dispossession, but not because they were old-fashioned. They were not religious conservatives confronting the sin of adultery. Had they been, they would have known how to forgive. Nor were they misplaced Victorians bound to traditional morality. Just the opposite. They had no objection when Catherine and I lived together for a decade before getting married; they were thrilled when Massachusetts allowed my sister to marry her partner. Their struggle was not about right and wrong, but about love and hatred. It was about identity, not morality.

Genesis tells us that without love, life would be overwhelmingly lonely. Adam and Eve are described as "two become one," which is as fine an image of love as we will ever find. Without Eve, Adam was by himself, and not even God's presence was enough to cure his loneliness. After Eve's arrival, not even the threat of divine punishment is enough to keep Adam from following Eve wherever she might lead him. For love, we will give up even paradise. Love leads us into a world that is both a part of us and more than us. Despite this promise of fulfillment, love is endlessly demanding. Raising children, sustaining a family, providing for the community by building a common world, these are the tasks that define a life well lived. They also require the labor that fills all of our days.

We can labor for only so long before we are exhausted at the end of the day and, finally, at the end of all of our days. Bound to the body, we are bound to labor, which both sustains us and kills us. For everyone, the burdens of labor can be just too much. When we forget love, as we all do at times, we experience daily life only as power. Sometimes, we think we have power over others, but mostly our experience is of the absence of power. We are, we feel, controlled by forces larger than ourselves. No matter where we stand, we are always overwhelmed by institutions, roles, and beliefs over which we have no control. We experience our lives as if we entered the middle of someone else's story; we can neither set our own beginning nor control our own end. This was how my father felt about life in suburbia. It was also the way my mother felt about life with him. He was controlling the narrative of their lives. They were living his script.

The attraction of the affair to my mother had, I suspect, less to do with a fantasy of romance and more to do with the power of the pornographic. Sexual revolution—the promise of free love—was in the air. Love, however, is never free; it often demands more than we can pay. Pornography, despite its commercialization, can be fundamentally about freedom. It can be an aspect of the carnivalesque inversion of power. This is the sexuality of the ecstatic moment, which is why there can be a fine line between religious ecstasy and the pornographic.

The pornographic strips sex of the burdens of ordinary life. It produces no children. It is not an ongoing task, but a singular performance. It sets forth an image of the body as complete in and of itself. The body is no longer the wasting asset that brings us to death. It is, instead, the source of self-transcendence, promising the completion that was present in the garden. The pornographic does not even require that social minimum of language.

Like religious ecstasy, the pornographic announces that the truth of the self—the authentic self—is not to be found in the endless demands of daily life. Because pornography so often appears as entertainment, we tend to confuse it with the pleasurable. Like other forms of the ecstatic, however, the pornographic can be painful. Its virtue is freedom, and freedom carries with it an idea of resistance overcome.

Paradoxically, the pornographic body is not really of this world. The pornographic moment is cut off from everything else. It can only be repeated; it cannot grow. It does not offer depth, but only more of the same. Life is represented as a series of such moments, not a process. We fantasize about the meeting of a stranger who comes as if from nowhere and disappears without leaving a trace. It could be anywhere; it could happen at any time. This unbounded quality is often represented by locating the pornographic moment during a trip. For my mother, I think it was the business trip.

The pornographic lives as memory and hope, but never more than that. It is not a space or time within which we can actually live. It is a comic fantasy for it promises freedom without effort. We need only strip off our clothes in order to find authenticity. As soon as discourse enters the pornographic, the fantasy of freedom within the limits of the body alone disappears. The pornographic, at that point, gives way to an ordinary morality tale of self-discovery and love. We literally cannot speak of the pornographic without turning it into its opposite.

The tale of the pornographic encounter becomes a tale of romance that ends, in one form or another, with "they lived happily ever after." Often the story is one in which the pornographic exchange makes possible a return to and regrounding of an existing relationship. Pornography becomes a kind of pilgrimage to a place where truth shows itself. Pilgrimage contains the idea of return: we travel beyond our borders in order to recover a new foundation. Thus, my mother's "I was lonely" converted the fantasy of the pornographic into a moment of relief within the path of her ordinary life. This is the moralizing of the ecstatic. It was what her therapist taught, but my father refused to hear.

I can understand how my mother was led to her affair. I suspect, however, that my mother was not very good at acting out the fantasy of the pornographic. Essential to that fantasy is the absence of speech. Pornography shares a speechlessness with the ecstatic. In both, speech becomes only a kind of talking in tongues. Could my mother cease her endless talk? One does not play Jewish geography with one's coconspirator in the pornographic. To do so would be to link the affair to intersecting narratives of families across time and space. There is no relief from the burdens of labor in that direction. Talk would only lead my mother back to my father, which is exactly where she always was.

My father had no interest in the pornographic fantasy of ecstatic completion. He did not believe that the body could promise relief from labor, that through the body he could find his way back to a lost paradise. He did not think there was any way back because he did not think there was anywhere to go. He saw in the body just one thing: the promise of death. Dying to the burdens of labor was for him dying plain and simple.

A person who cannot forget the looming presence of death cannot achieve that timelessness that is the promise of the pornographic. That promise, had my father thought of it, would have struck him as silly—as silly as the idea that religion could save him from death. He was as deeply committed an atheist as I have ever met. He revolted at the very idea of hope. Without hope, we will come to hate all that reminds us of death. My father now saw death all around him and he was filled with hate.

Either we have faith in the possibility of love in and through the other, or we are lost. Plato invented a myth to explain love; he got this point just right. Once, we were circlemen, rolling around with eight limbs. For our sins, the gods struck us in two. Love is the endless longing to be rejoined with one's other half. This captures, better even than the image of the two-become-one of Adam and Eve, the promise of unity and completeness with the beloved. Plato offers a comic account of completion when true lovers are joined back together. They want only what they have: union. They do not speak and do not reproduce. They do not labor at all. They are literally dead to ordinary life—a mythic representation of the link between pornography and the ecstatic.

My father found himself imagining his other half—my mother— joined to someone else. He suffered his own body as a gaping wound ripped apart from its other half. If she had been complete, then he was nothing. If he had been a religious person in an earlier age, he would have been led to self-flagellation. If he had succeeded in his denials, he would have walked away from my mother. Instead, he remained locked in place, suffering an unbearable pain.

We cannot understand love without taking seriously Plato's myth of the circlemen. It tells us that love is not a mutually beneficial relationship; it is not a deal, but a condition. Love promises the completion of the self through the other. We want to possess and be possessed. We cannot do without this mythical moment of completion, in which we are released from the burdens of labor and the threat of death. We want to cease talking and just be in that moment. As soon as speech returns, we are drawn back into the everyday world of family, friends, politics, and labor.

Lovers can be—perhaps must be—co-conspirators in the pornographic. They make complete and total claims upon each other. They do not bargain; there is no place for ideas of a just measure. In the face of one's other half, one wants endlessly and without measure. This is why the action of love is sacrifice: it is always a giving up of the self for the sake of that mythical union that is the only truth that matters to the lovers.

My father felt desperately the pain of rejection by my mother. However, he was and had always been quite incapable of sacrifice. He knew the body only as the threat of death, not as the promise of completion. But it would be wrong to think that this meant that he did not love my mother. She was his other half. He was in love but incapable of the action of love. This was pretty much his relationship to his children as well. In the next chapter, I explore the sources of my father's disability. My father, no less than my mother, was a product of the trauma of the twentieth century. For her, it began with flight from German genocide against the Jews; for him, it began with the Great Depression and then the War.

As I think back on my parents' life, I see that I am not a child of the sixties at all. That was a time in which starting over could seem a virtue of authenticity. If we are each responsible for our own life, we may fail to take responsibility for others. Responsibility and irresponsibility must have seemed terribly confused to my parents. Both of them were too busy trying to figure out the meaning of authenticity to think much about anybody else. Free love really meant free sex for there was not much love to go around. Can there be such a thing as a loveless age?

My life has been set deeply and directly against this idea of individual self-creation. At the center of all that I do and all that I think is the fact of love. I have argued and fought against the idea that our lives become meaningful through the decisions that we make. Even when we bring to those decisions all of the skills of forethought of which we are capable, it is not enough. Deliberation and reason are not the sources of a meaningful life. Meaning explodes into one's life from outside. It comes to us as an act of grace. It grabs hold and tells us who we are regardless of what we might have thought or how we might have chosen. My parents were acting out. They were exploring; they were not called.

Love is all that we can hold on to and it comes at us always in the same way as the newborn child. It comes from outside of our ordinary world, but it fully and completely tells us who we are. This view of love makes me a religious person, although I hold no conventional religious beliefs. I am too much my father's son for that. But I know what the saints and prophets were talking about: the need for grace in our lives and the absolute loneliness of death without that grace. My mother felt this need when she reached seventy-five, but by then it was too late.

My parents were children not just of the era of Roosevelt, but of that of The Beatles. This is what the comedy of Capt'n Sam was all about: rebellion and authenticity. My mother longed to make the same statement as my father. The affair had been her authentic moment. She wanted the world to know who she had been; she certainly wanted him to know. Thus, she was led to the confession. No less than my father, she insisted on a tale of self-discovery. "Yes, I said yes." But what they thought they knew of life turned out to be no more substantial than my mother's imagination or my father's donning of a captain's cap. Somehow, the twentieth century had brought them to a loveless world. In that world, whatever love they had for each other was lost to carelessness and then turned to hate.

My parents did not survive the sixties. Not the Depression, not the War, not even the Holocaust did them in. They were destroyed by the sixties and the belief that each of us must construct an authentic life for ourselves. That is the short of it. The missing photos, the lost past, the endless chatter, and the declarations were all about the absence of a love that knows no beginning and no end. Each wanted to be free; each ended up destroying the other. The sixties were supposed to be comedy, but all they produced for my parents was tragedy. Maybe comedy and tragedy really are one and the same in the end.

Chapter Two

Memory

My father suffered from post-traumatic stress disorder, or PTSD. I did not understand this until late in his life. It was never formally diagnosed, but I am confident in my judgment. He never realized what it was that was wrong with him. He thought he saw the world honestly; it was just a terrible place. The one quality that he lacked, above all others, was self-understanding. Mostly, he could not bear to look at himself. When he did think about himself, he usually thought about other people and how awful they were. He always appeared to himself as the victim or potential victim.

I only came to see the centrality of PTSD to his life after I got involved in a neuroethics program at the university. The program included medical researchers from the nearby Veterans Administration hospital. From them, I began to hear about the problems of veterans who could never leave their wartime experience behind. Those patients had suffered a breakdown in the working of memory. Not that ordinary breakdown of old age, which is forgetting. Just the opposite: they could not forget images of war. Stuck, they could not return to civilian life and the ordinary pursuits of family and work.

That many men cannot successfully manage the return home after visiting the killing fields has always been common knowledge. Until recently, however, no one wanted to talk about these damaged men. They were collateral damage. Their problems were personal matters— "nerves" or "shell shock." Such men were thought to display a weakness of character; they were not "man" enough to deal with war. Knowledge of their condition was kept within the family.

Our family was no better at dealing with the problem my father posed. We all knew there was something deeply wrong, but no one wanted to talk about it. What, after all, would have been the point? He was not going to admit he had a problem or seek professional help. Part of his problem was that he was unable to think of himself as someone who needed help. In his view, he was fine; the problem was in everyone else. We had no idea of what to do for him. So, we did nothing.

Even if we did not speak of it, my father was certainly one of the war-damaged. I know now that his family thought him very much changed when he came back from the War. He had left a "sweet child" of nineteen, who had already graduated from college. He came back angry and unsettled. His efforts at reintegration after the War repeatedly failed. He seemed to be always in flight—moving across the country as he changed jobs and professions. He was, unfortunately, fleeing from something that he could not leave behind: memory.

He finally escaped from an incapacitating memory of war when he found his own peaceful idyll on the Chesapeake. He needed a life in which he was accountable to no one and in which he did not have to compete with anyone. Thanks to the 1960s, he almost achieved it. Abandonment of suburban life became not only legitimate but also heroic. He could tell himself that he was not in flight, but rather was choosing authenticity. For fifteen years, he found pretty much what he wanted: to be invisible. He did not have to give an account of himself to anyone. Then, there was my mother's confession. It made him again unbearably visible to himself. It was a new trauma, and it had much the same effects as the earlier experience of combat. It filled his imagination; he could not get it out of his mind. Once again, he was suffering from PTSD.

That men could be permanently damaged, rather than strengthened, by surviving battle does not exactly fit into the heroic myth of the West. An entire culture has been built around the idea of courageous defense of polity and home. Did classical Greeks, when they came back from battling the Persians, suffer from PTSD? What about our own Revolutionary War heroes? Did some come back from Yorktown broken men, unable to move forward with their lives, stuck forever in the scenes of death and destruction? The answer must be, "yes indeed." PTSD has been the underside of the warrior's courage for as long as there have been people killing each other, which is for as long as there have been people.

In the neuroethics group, I heard a good deal about investigations into the biological foundation of PTSD. Many researchers think it to be a consequence of a neurological condition. If that is so, it has always been with us. It may even be that the percentage of the population with the condition is constant. It just seems more prevalent today, because we are now willing to talk about it. The suffering veteran is no longer an unpleasant family secret but a problem for medical science. Research is funded and treatment protocols are generated. I suspect this change in attitudes has something to do with the end of conscription and the political embrace of the Vietnam veteran after the success of the anti-war movement. A conscript army lives on the idea that everyone can serve as a citizen-soldier. Reconciliation after Vietnam meant casting the soldier as a victim of misdirected politics. He, too, needs our care.

For the suffering victims, there has been a great benefit in psychotherapy's turn away from talking cures and toward the investigation of the neurological sources of this disorder. Ironically, identifying PTSD as a physical condition allows us to talk about it more easily. It strips the condition out of the ethos of courage and shame. A moral failing is transformed into a treatable, neurological condition. Those who bear this physical condition should never have been sent to war. When they return, they should be treated as among the war wounded. My father was indeed one of the wounded, even if he could not see his own injury.

That his behavior could be linked to his army service had never occurred to me. No one had ever mentioned the possibility. I wonder now if my mother ever had that thought. What did she think about the absence of war buddies or the silence about his war experience? Unfortunately, by the time I learned about PTSD, it was too late in his life. The war had been long ago. Whatever the sources of his character, he had become that person whom we knew. One does not get to redo a life.

My father, of course, never thought of himself as ill. Mostly, his condition remained a family secret. Others knew that he had a temper and that he had a tendency toward harsh judgments. They did not know about the uncontrollable anger, the deep fears, the sleeplessness, the cold sweats, and the constant flight.

Labeling PTSD as a neurological condition helps to relieve the victim of his sense of guilt and of moral failure. Performance in combat is, after all, about as close to the traditional male virtues as one can get. A failure there is no small matter. True, PTSD may show itself only after the trauma of combat is over. It does not signal anything at all about military conduct or performance. However, the nature of PTSD is to blur the line between the event and the memory of the event. Recall of the threat of death and injury takes over the workings of the imagination. At that point, what actually happened does not matter. After my mother's confession, my father could not distinguish between the fact of the affair and his imagining of the affair. Imagining the affair, it was fully present.

The neurological explanation of PTSD is not just a theory, but also a first step in treatment. It alters the moral valence of PTSD, even as pharmacological interventions seek to alter the memory itself. If it is neurological, we can assure the victim that his suffering is only his misfortune, not his fault. He has a malfunctioning brain that will not let his imagination free itself of the battlefield. With this shift of perspective, completely new possibilities of treatment open up. These options raised ethical issues that the neuroscientists wanted to discuss with me.

The doctors had no problem with the pursuit of drugs that could relieve the condition, but what about the idea of screening for the syndrome in advance? As with everything else biological, there may be genetic markers indicating a proclivity for the syndrome. Just as one can be too short or too heavy for the military, perhaps one can have a memory function that disqualifies one for service. Is such screening ethically appropriate in a democratic political order? If we can screen, what about treatment in advance—a kind of vaccine against PTSD? Should we aim to make it possible for every individual to experience combat in a "normal" way? Can we think of combat as occupying a normal place in memory?

Medical intervention to improve memory is something many people desire. If such treatment exists, it may be morally questionable to fail to make it available in the same way as treatments for other disorders are available. Would not such a treatment be a boon to the elderly? What about interventions to eliminate memory? If it is truthful memory, what exactly are we doing? Do we really want to intervene to eliminate painful memories? The range of painful memories is hardly limited to those of war. This begins to sound more like science fiction than healthcare. Quickly, we begin to imagine the political possibilities that can attach to the manipulation of memory.

Our ordinary lives are made possible as much by forgetting as by memory. Sometimes it seems that, at this point in my life, for every new item I remember, I must pay the cost of forgetting something. It is a zero-sum game. This balancing of remembering and forgetting begins well before we reach the limits of our capacity for memory. We need to free the present of the past in order to make room for new experience. Too much of such freedom, however, and we can no longer make sense of who we are. As with so many other things, of memory too there is a right proportion between retaining and forgetting.

PTSD disturbs this balance. It is a sort of inverse image of amnesia. There, forgetting becomes unbound; here, memory overwhelms. When we treat forgetting, we know what we are doing. We want to remember what we have done; we want to remember those people and events that have made us who we are. The tragedy of Alzheimer's disease is that the victim literally forgets her own life; she loses the narrative that is herself. But at what are we aiming when we seek to treat too much memory? There is no easy measure of the appropriate amount of forgetting, when it is the truth from which we suffer. My mother may have tended toward fiction in the operation of her memory. My father suffered from the thing itself. It was what he had seen and felt that he could not forget.

When we talk about PTSD, we are never quite sure what normal should be. Only from the point of view of modern medicine is it obvious that PTSD is a disorder at all. If normal suggests any kind of value judgment, what exactly is the right way to react to the experience of battle? To see the bodies of friends torn apart, to see the things that we are willing to do to each other for the sake of something as insubstantial as a political idea, is to see something very dark indeed. Should we ever forget this? To go mad may be the only honest response to this sight. There is a reason that Shakespeare's fools always seem to know more than everybody else. They hide, but do not forget, what they know.

Treating PTSD as an organic disorder, we are relieved of having to think about any of the deeper questions regarding the meaning of life in the face of suffering and death. I was not invited to talk to the neuroscientists because they were concerned with the meaning of life. No matter how I might try, this was not a direction in which they had any interest in going. Their ethical concerns were far more local. In their view, there is only one appropriate response to pain: to seek its relief. Suffering may once have been a sign of truth—think of Jesus on the cross—but it is no longer. Now, it is a condition to be alleviated. We want to medicalize everything above or below normal. Too much energy is a symptom, and so is too little. To prove the point, we have a whole generation of children raised on Ritalin. Similarly, too much memory is the symptom of PTSD. The doctors imagined a Ritalin for memory.

Just as we no longer think that truth should be painful, we no longer associate madness with insight. Prophecy was always disturbingly close to madness. Now, it has gone over the line. Anyone who claims to be a prophet today is a candidate for treatment. Yet, for a long time the mad were thought to know something. They could see better than the rest of us. One of the things they knew is that we can injure and kill each other for no reason at all—or at least no reason that can stand a moment's scrutiny. For two generations, we were threatening the Soviets and they were threatening us. Somehow, two economic theories—capitalism and communism—had become the axis around which we formed ideas of good and evil. Over the issue of who should own the means of production, each side risked world destruction. No one really understood how this happened or why. At least the mad can see the madness in it.

In war, we hate the enemy and are willing to kill with great fury. Peace is declared and quickly we find we could not be closer friends with the same people. The Germans and the Japanese have been our closest allies for seventy years. This must have seemed altogether puzzling to my father and his generation. For years, he would not return to Germany. Neither would my mother. However, in 1961, they went. They found it interesting rather than scandalous. Life had gone on. It might be enough to drive a person mad, if he continued to dwell on his own past efforts to kill these very people, or on what they had done to his friends and companions. My father did not bear grudges; he did not continue to fight his own private war. Yet, in the war, he had been to the edge of madness and he certainly had trouble returning.

The traumatized veteran refuses to get on with his life. He remains forever in the shock of the discovery of the madness of the battlefield. We can think of this as a sort of private act of bearing witness. The problem is that the veteran with PTSD is bearing this testimony only to himself. He is his own audience, staring forever in disbelief at what he has seen and what he has done. If he is sane, he is certainly not normal. I know my father was not normal. Whether he was insane is a more difficult question. Carrying on in the midst of the memory of the unbearable requires either more power than he had or less power than he had. Is it weakness of the will or strength of character that makes it possible to cope with the unbearable?

What is unthinkable is the image of the body being treated as something to be disposed of, as if no longer part of the human world. War creates such trauma not just because it threatens injury. Many activities and conditions do that. Unique to war is the way in which it becomes entirely ordinary to treat the destruction of the body as if it were merely an object. Imagine if you were repeatedly confronted with an image of yourself on the embalmer's table. The western front of the Second World War was that table and my father's imagination was seized with that image. All he could do was to repeat endlessly to himself, "The horror, the horror."

Surely the refusal to move on makes as much sense as the lawyer's response of writing rules for who can kill whom in the hell of war—mostly young men killing each other. How anyone could look out at the devastation of a field of battle and think that it presents a problem for legal ordering is more than a little puzzling. No one looked at the concentration camps and thought that the problem was to create a legal order specifying who could be starved to death and who could be gassed. Actually, that is not true. There certainly was a German administrative mentality that had just that reaction. Think of Eichmann. It is just that those who thought this way lost the war. The winners distinguish between the administrative murder of the camps and the romance of battle.

There is some undeniable insanity in this. Politics may insist that there are good deaths and bad deaths, but the mad know better. They know that there is only the one death for each of us. Regardless of what the state may say, we each die our own death, just as we each live our own lives. This was my father: he was certain that he must die a singular death and nothing in this life was going to change that. He could not forget this basic truth, but he had no resources with which to confront it. Without faith in the gods or others, what might those resources have been? He needed the relief of forgetting, but the doctors did not yet have any drug on offer.

The neuroscientists and doctors I met from the Veterans Administration Hospital were all well-meaning people intent on bringing some relief to their patients. All were committed to a physiological model of the disorder. Thinking about my father, however, makes me question the adequacy of this model to really understand what it is to suffer from PTSD. What is it that allows men to face the insanity of battle, to expose themselves to death and injury? It surely cannot be a theory of the state, as if they had read Locke on human rights or Hobbes on the social contract. We do not sacrifice ourselves for abstract ideas of justice, let alone for economic theories. There is plenty of injustice in the world, but for the most part, we have "no dog in those fights," as an old mentor of mine used to say. Only one thing allows men to accept the idea of their own sacrifice: love. It may be love of country; it may be love of one's companions on the battlefield; it may be love of family. A life in the embrace of love will find a common thread running through all of these relationships: from family, to friends, to state. We sacrifice for love or we flee from death.

The memory of the carnage of battle puts this question: Do we see in that memory the threat of death or the act of sacrifice? Lincoln looked at the killing fields of Gettysburg and saw sacrifice; he saw sacred ground consecrated by war. What did the veterans themselves see? When Lincoln spoke, the battlefield was still rank from the unburied bodies. Did the veterans share Lincoln's view that here they had touched the sacred or did they see only death and the threat of death? They must have asked themselves, "How much is it worth?" Lincoln surely worried that they would choose flight and with that an untimely settlement with the South.

This question of love or death has haunted the West at least since Christianity founded faith on the experience of the cross. Can we see in Christ's death sacrifice or do we see only the murder of a carpenter at the hands of the state? Love or death? This is the question posed by the memory of war. My father saw death. That is what he could not forget. That memory led to endless flight.

Those who suffer from PTSD may have a neurological problem, but it displays itself to those close to them as a failure of love. Yet perhaps this gets the order wrong. Should we say rather that the victims suffer from a failure of love, which shows itself in certain effects upon the body, including neurological effects? Which approach we take depends upon what we are trying to do. If we want to build an effective military, genetic screening for the markers of PTSD is certainly more useful than exploring the nature of love. If we want to understand those to whom we are bound in our own relationships of care, then we need to explore the soul and the capacity for love.

Just as scientists pursue the genetic disposition for PTSD, thinking about my father persuades me that there is a moral disposition in this direction. If PTSD is a failure of love, then surely it makes sense to ask how it was that he imagined himself and his relationship to the world before the image of battle ever grabbed hold of his imagination. He found himself in a loveless world well before he went to war. If the action of love is the giving up of the self for another—sacrifice—then my father could not find in himself a capacity for love. This incapacity unsuited him for war. Some might say his ego was too big; others, his fear of death too large. I would say that he was a person without a single religious impulse. Without any sort of faith, there was only himself in a losing battle with the world. To me, he constantly posed the question of whether we can face death without love. The answer was always the same: without love, we are indeed lost.

My father's most basic attitude toward the world was one of resentment. His resentment had come early and ran deep and strong. It was, for him, a metaphysical position; it reflected his view of the very nature of existence. He resented the entire world and his place in it. Life, as he saw it, was endless injustice. Tracing the origins of this view, I am speculating about events I never saw and things about which he never talked. Still, I am confident of my account. It is true in the same way my mother's memory of her affair was true: a truth beyond the merely factual. Imagining my father, I am writing the narrative that gives voice to his life—at least as I knew it. This is the only kind of history that makes a difference in the end: the histories we create in order to make sense of the people we find in our lives.

It would be easy to think that my father's resentment was a consequence of the unfortunate circumstances of his early life. His father died suddenly when he was two. I am sure he never got over the loss. Anyone would resent the absence of a father; more so, if he suddenly disappeared. As with the rest of his past, he never spoke of his childhood. Perhaps this was the absence that dominated everything, just like the war was the presence that never ended. His father's death produced his belief in the fundamental injustice of the world; the war produced an inescapable experience of angst. This was my father: furious at the injustice he suffered, and raging at his own mortality. In both respects, he cast himself as victim. He was always alone at the center of a world that threatened either to abandon him or to kill him.

A psychoanalyst friend tells me that my father's early loss of his own father must be the key to all that followed. Abandoned by his father, he could no longer trust anyone. Every relationship throughout his life would reflect this fear of loss. No one could be trusted; love meant pain. This early trauma, according to the psychoanalyst, was enough to establish a permanent attitude of resentment. No doubt, it was important, but one must also take account of the historical moment and the other circumstances of his family. My response to the psychoanalyst is the same as my response to the neuroscientists: a life cannot be explained through a single dimension.

Born in 1923, my father arrived just early enough in the century to know a life of some wealth. That was twice wiped out: first with his father's death and then with the Great Depression. Of the first, he had no memory; of the second, he remembered a good deal. His family had been relatively well off. His father ran a wholesale meat business. My father had a very vague memory of a nice home in New York, before the family's collapse. Mostly, however, he remembered poverty. He lived in a small apartment with his mother and two older siblings. His older sister was sixteen when their father died. She went to work to support the family. Other relatives helped.

Many people, including those who had been wealthy, make it through economic hard times without taking it personally. Children, in particular, are malleable. They can find excitement and adventure in change, even if it seems to older people a change for the worse. My father's resentment stemmed not from the facts of loss alone, but from the way in which his family survived. The loss of his father and then the Depression made him and his mother dependent on the kindness of others. This is what he absolutely could not stand.

Despite the Depression, he grew up quite spoiled, thanks to his mother and his older sister. He was the golden boy, the brilliant child who could do no wrong. He had high expectations for himself and made demands on others. He entered City College at fifteen and was done by nineteen—in time to go to war with a bachelor's degree in chemistry. That degree was close enough to medicine that he was assigned the role of medic. Perhaps that assignment saved his life. It also shaped his imagination.

Growing up in a household of women who hovered over him, sexism was an inseparable part of who he was. Would the presence of a father have made a difference? Surely, his father would not have taught him a lesson of gender equality within the home. It was not yet a part of the culture and his father was, I am told, a loud, dominating male. Still, I cannot help but think that there was something childlike in his relationship to my mother. He remained the spoiled, favorite child; he was deeply selfish.

When young, his mother and sister constantly told him that he was special. He grew up believing he was the smartest person in the room and that this made him better than others. He was, therefore, more deserving. He carried this conviction throughout his life. Even as he was told that he was special, he saw that everything he needed came from others who could withdraw their support at any time. The world was not in sync, for reward did not match merit.

His father's death had thrown the family on the good will of relatives. There was no life insurance; there could not have been much in savings. My grandmother, who was only forty-two when her husband died, must have fallen apart. She had worked briefly as a young woman, before marrying the much older boss—my grandfather. After his death, she did not return to work. She lived into her nineties, but never worked again. Not wanting to cause anyone any problems, she withdrew. The result was they became wholly dependent upon others.

My father resented his mother's failure to provide. More than that, he resented her failure to take command of their lives. In his view, she could do nothing. She could neither provide care nor take care. That she was dealing with the loss of a husband and then the Great Depression would not have registered on a child. She had not wanted to impose herself on others, but their entire lives became an imposition. My father never reconciled himself to this. Out of this grew his insistence on justice, by which he meant each should get that to which he or she is entitled. Out of this as well came his visceral dislike of the very idea of charity.

My father would tell us the story of how his mother could not cook. Opening a can of peas, he said, was as far as she could get. I do not know whether the story is true; I have no memories of her in a kitchen. I am sure, however, that cooking was the least of the matter. Cooking stood for home; it stood for taking care, for security in an insecure time. There was no counterbalancing story of what it was that she could do. The can of peas stood as much for their poverty as for culinary ability. The peas were all she could cook because it was all she could afford. Even when they lived in their own apartment, meals were literally brought to them by relatives who lived close by. Perhaps there were other butchers in the extended family and they were providing leftovers from the store. This dependence was the fundamental fact for which my father never forgave her.

His adult relationships with most of his other relatives were not much better. He was determined to be independent of all of them. He judged them and most failed his test. The most spectacular failure was not his mother, but his brother. My father was by far the youngest child of three. His brother was some eight years older; his sister six years older still. In my father's early years, he must have associated his older brother with his absent father, for the resentment he felt toward his brother was deep and unforgiving. Perhaps he expected his brother to step into the paternal role, but he failed to do so. Perhaps he just resented that his brother got out of the house, leaving him alone with his mother.

There was always something shadowy about my father's account of what his brother actually did. Something perhaps at the edge of the law? Whatever it was, it did not involve taking responsibility for my father and their mother. My father never forgave him. For the rest of their lives, they barely spoke to each other. That entire side of the family was subject to his derision. As far as he was concerned, his brother's sin had corrupted the blood. His nephew and niece, and then their entire families, were subject to the same sort of derision. I saw them only at funerals and weddings.

After his sister married, my father and his mother were supported in a small New York apartment by his new brother-in-law. My grandmother would eventually move in with her daughter and husband, when my father left for the War. This is where and how I knew her when I was a child. After the war, my father lived with his sister's family as well, while he went to MIT. That my uncle accepted the burden of his new wife's family made him the only saint in my father's entire family tree. Among the diverse careers that my father pursued over the course of his life, one was that of a patent attorney. Not coincidentally, his brother-in-law was a patent attorney. There was at least one role model in my father's life. My uncle, however, was a very modest man without resentment and without the experience of war. He could only model so much for my father, who seethed with uncontrollable thoughts and emotions. Like his other career choices, this one did not last.

If my father's attitude toward his brother bordered on hatred, his attitude toward his sister was a much softer form of resentment. She really had saved the family, dropping out of school to support everyone after the death of their father. Nevertheless, my father was less appreciative than resentful of the fact that he had to be saved. Rather than recognize his resentment for what it was, she made excuses for him. Always it was the same excuse: smart children are difficult children. I thought the excuse made no sense, since she had a daughter who was both smart and nice.

My father was convinced that he deserved more than others, even as he resented being dependent upon others. He held on to both of these beliefs for the whole of his life. He could not tolerate being judged because he thought he was better—meaning smarter—than everybody else. He was to be judge, not judged. His keen sense of injustice was the reverse side of his resentment. In a just world, he would not be dependent on others. He would be recognized for what he was: special. Since he could not blame the gods for all the injustice he suffered, he could only blame others. He tended to blame everyone.

I do not remember ever hearing my father thank anyone. It was impossible for him to acknowledge care freely given. Indeed, he could not stand the idea that someone might do something for him as an act of kindness. He had no problem with making demands on others, but always as a matter of what he thought to be right. He did not think that he should thank people for that which they had an obligation to do. He never thanked service people. Service, after all, was their job. He did not want anything that reminded him of charity, which meant he was careful to pay his bills. Fortunately for him—or unfortunately—those who lack kindness rarely have anything kind done for them. His behavior did not prompt generous behavior in turn.

Nor can I remember him ever asking for help, at least not until he was very old. He could hire help. He believed he should treat those who worked for him justly. He wanted to pay a fair wage. He was not interested in cheating anyone. The other side of this, however, was that he thought his employees should treat him fairly, which meant that they should do what justice required. He resented having to tell them what to do. He thought that unfairly put the burden on him. He was continually disappointed in his employees, who did not share his acute sense of justice. He thought they were taking advantage of him, when actually they were not thinking of him at all. Just as he was not much of a boss, he was not much of a capitalist. Had he made a profit with his small business, he would have thought he should share the wealth with his two employees. He told them this when he first took over the business. I doubt they believed him, or maybe they already knew there would be no profit. My father's moral universe was, then, an odd mixture of ideas of equality and inequality. Justice made everyone equal, but only he managed the burden of justice properly. He was more equal than everyone else and thus more deserving.

Life at home, he thought, should operate on the same principles as his business. These were, after all, the principles of his moral universe. He could demand—not ask—that I do something, but not because he was trying to teach the obligations of care or a generosity of spirit. For him, it was always a matter of justice, meaning this is what is owed as a matter of familial obligation: cut the grass. Since it was an obligation of justice, he should not have to ask. Even a teenager should notice when the grass needs mowing. A failure of initiative on my part was an injustice. Not to do something when it was evident that it needed to be done was always a moral failure. The moralizing extended into the most trivial of acts: put your glass in the sink. About such failures, he could explode, for he saw in them an effort to take advantage of him. The entire world, even his family, threatened him with injustice. So he taught me the single moral principle that guided his life: there are only fuckers and fuckees in this world.

There were moments when his resentment produced genuine crises. There was, for example, the time, at age eight, that it almost killed me. I had entered a period in which I would wake up in the middle of the night, scared. I would go to seek safety from my parents. After several nights of this, my father exploded. In the middle of the night, he ran around the house screaming, "If I have to be up, then everybody has to be up." He turned on the television and the radio at their highest volume. He woke my siblings, who were as terrified as I was. So much for safety. I never bothered my parents again in the middle of the night. Shortly thereafter, however, my nighttime awakenings were accompanied by a pain in my gut. I was not about to wake my father. Very late, I was rushed to the hospital for an emergency appendectomy. The only mention my father ever made of this whole episode was to say that he supposed my earlier awakenings had been caused by my impending appendicitis. It was, therefore, not really my fault that I was waking him up. If it was not my fault, then his outburst was not his fault—at least this was the logic I inferred. No apology, just rationalization. I never told him that I continued to wake up after I got back from the hospital. The lesson I had learned was that he was not a man to be trusted.

I thought of this episode quite a bit when my second daughter was an infant. She was a child of high energy. She never slept more than four hours at a stretch until she reached 18 months. Often, deep in the night, I found myself sitting in a big chair in her room with her in my lap. She would be crying, on the edge of hysteria. I would repeat a simple mantra to myself, "This is a privilege." I would not be my father's son. Catherine and my older daughter would sleep soundly through the night.

My father viewed parenthood through the same frame of resentment with which he saw the rest of his life. He resented an eight-year-old child who stole his sleep. His actions are not explained by the ordinary sexism of the American family of the 1950s. Rather, that ordinary pattern hid the deeper forces at work in him. This became clear when the 1960s arrived. Now, the ordinary forms of authority were challenged, including his role as male, head of household. The leading value was no longer authority, but authenticity. Authenticity, for my father, had very little to do with care for anybody else. More than anything else, his attitude seemed one of relief that the burdens of parenting were over.

I remember in 1968, when I was sixteen, telling him that I planned to spend the summer hitchhiking around Europe with a friend—it was a safer time. His reaction was explosive. Why should I be able to do this while he was stuck at work? Where was the justice in this? Why was it not clear to me that I was taking advantage of him? It was not exactly jealousy; it was resentment at the injustice of his life. I went anyway. He may not have been able to free himself from home in the middle of the Depression, but I was growing up in the sixties. I was not bound to home and, after a little while, he was not going to remain bound either.

Just as he never wanted to be in a position in which he would have to thank someone, I do not remember any instance in which he did something out of simple kindness. The idea that he might donate time to a community organization or donate his skills as a lawyer simply did not cross his mind. I know exactly what he would have said to the suggestion: these are services that the poor deserve as a matter of justice, which means that the government should provide them. Public taxes and redistribution were the answer, not charitable acts. He never objected to paying his taxes. I do not disagree with his socialist leanings, but there remains the issue of character. He saw the world in terms of justice, not kindness or care. That may work, somewhere and sometimes, as a political program, but it is not the ground for a life rich with personal connections. He had none.

Even the camaraderie of the war did not create in him feelings of friendship and generosity. No war buddies ever showed up at our home. None was ever even spoken of. Instead, the war bred in him more resentment. He was smart, not brave. Courage is not an adjective that comes to mind when I think of him. He would not have put himself out for anyone, let alone for a political idea. His politics were on the left. His fundamental distinction of the fuckers from the fuckees was an echo of the socialist vision of a world of conflict between employers and workers. Despite his leftist leanings, it never occurred to him to join a march or a demonstration. He was, in his own mind, exceptional, while such political demonstrations were for ordinary people.

I never saw him take a physical risk, unless one counts a long habit of forgetting to put on his seat belt. It is not that he was a timid man. Around him, there was always a kind of turbulence. But whatever battles he was fighting, they were his alone, and he fought them entirely in his own head. He never joined groups of any kind. He easily angered, but it was not the sort of anger that triggered action. He did not join movements, let alone start them. His anger did not lead him out into the world. Instead, he was inclined to stew. He could stew for days on end. Sometimes, it would end in an explosion; sometimes, he simply lost the energy to continue.

Justice detached from action is not a virtue. What looked to him like a demand for justice looked to me like nothing more than an expression of resentment. He was not moved to action by injustices to others. For the most part, he simply did not care about others. It was not a misplaced demand for justice that kept him from acting with kindness. It was his resentment. He did not think that others had what they deserved; he could see the injustice. It just was not his responsibility. Why should he have to take on the burden of curing someone else's problem?

There was no good Samaritan in him. A person who does not show care will, in the end, fail at justice as well. There is a bumper sticker that says, "Perform random acts of kindness." My father was more inclined toward random acts of evil, particularly as he got older. He would tell stories of practical jokes he had performed on strangers. There was nothing funny in them, just a pathetic malevolence. He once told the mother of a child feeding bread to ducks that bread had been found to cause the death of the birds. He did this because he thought it terrible that the ducks would congregate to be fed, leaving their droppings all over the area in which people liked to walk. That the droppings were a mess should, he thought, have been obvious to everyone. Mother and child were acting unjustly. Resentment was his response. His was a world without sympathy or kindness.

In all of his interactions with people, there was an edge of loneliness: him against the world. He thought people should take responsibility for themselves. Do not impose yourself on others; do your share; do it without being told. No reason to do more than your share. These were the rules of his moral life. There was nothing here about kindness, generosity, or love. He was chronically disappointed in people because no one ever met his standard of justice. But for my mother, I doubt anyone would have had much to do with him.

My father always thought he knew more than anyone else did. He possessed that characteristic belief of the mad in the absolute truth of their own insights. Whatever he saw, that was exactly the way the world was. This was a man who resisted wearing glasses until very late in life. Not because his eyesight was uniquely good. Rather, whatever he saw had to be the truth. Like his quip about my mother, "rarely right, but never uncertain," he too was never uncertain. His emotional insight, unfortunately, was about as good as his eyesight. He believed that whatever he did not see was not there. There was, however, a good deal that simply escaped his vision.

Most importantly, he could not stand to look at himself. For a long time he would not visit doctors. To go to a doctor is to think of oneself as a vulnerable body that needs care. After the War, he could not look at himself in this way. Well into his eighties, he broke his arm. A visiting nurse was assigned to come check on him and get him going with some physical therapy. He quickly went through several nurses. He would drive them away with his rudeness. The problem here was not that he could not accept charity. They were all paid for their work. Rather, he refused to recognize them, because he refused to acknowledge his own physical need. He was unable even to speak politely to them. Eventually, they simply gave up. He thought he could cure himself by sitting still. As long as he was not moving, his broken arm would not register as a problem. This was his general approach to all forms of therapy, including exercise: better to sit still, for strenuous movement would only announce the body's frailty. That which he did not see did not exist.

My father could not stand being the object of anyone's observation. He did not want to be looked at; he did not want to be examined. He could not stand any of this because the thought that he was a living—and therefore a dying body—was intolerable. To be examined by the doctor reminded him too much of the cadaver that he will become: laid out flat on the table of an undertaker. To be invisible, on the other hand, was to be immortal. If he could not be invisible, he could at least be unobserved. Perhaps, in some odd way, he thought that death would not be able to find him, if he stayed out of sight.

I have known people who seek to be invisible by occupying as little space as possible. They withdraw into themselves and hide within baggy clothing. This was not my father. He was by no means a meek man. He filled a lot of space. Still, he could not tolerate being observed. His response to this contradiction was not to hide, but to suppress the idea that there might be anything of interest in his body. He seemed indifferent to nudity, his own or anyone else's. If he had enjoyed being with others more, he might have joined a nudist colony. Except he never joined anything. "Member" was not a term he could apply to himself.

I never heard him express any interest in the erotic. He might make fun of the young women sunbathing on the beach at the marina—he enjoyed crude jokes—but not with even a hint of interest in them. No hidden magazines or pictures at home or in the shop. He presented himself as a thoroughly modern individual, who lived in a world of bodies emptied of mystery. In fact, he was not this at all. Modern people go to doctors. Nor was it some sort of commitment to feminism or to gender equality. He never expressed any sympathy for feminism and had the misogynist beliefs typical of most men of his generation. There was nothing political or moral in any of this. Nor was it about my mother, from whom I suspect he had already withdrawn physically. He was alone at the center of his world.

For him, the body was to be treated as if it were nothing at all. It did not need care: no doctors. It did not promise pleasure: no sex. It did not threaten death: no visibility. He might seem like a free-spirited nudist, but it was not because he valued the natural. Just the opposite, he had no interest in it whatsoever. He was unmoved by the wild, unenthusiastic about environmentalism. He liked to sail because of the solitude, not because of the vistas of the open sea and spectacular sunsets. His apparent openness about the body had nothing to do with connecting with nature, but everything to do with denying the human significance of the natural. He may have taken advantage of the sixties to flee from suburban life, but he remained a man of the forties most of all. The War set the pattern of his life.

My father was hiding in plain sight. This combination of visibility and invisibility, of hiding while being present, may seem odd, until one thinks about how soldiers live and die. The soldier is uniquely visible. War is an environment that absolutely denies privacy. The soldier is ordered to expose himself to injury and risk, even though his instinct must be to flee and to hide. The idea of the mystery of the body, the body as an expression of the erotic, must be driven away. This is the point of basic training. There are no hidden mysteries in the foxhole. None in the barracks either, for that matter. The combatant lives in an entirely public world but hopes he will not be noticed. He does not want to be seen by the enemy; he does not want to be seen by his superiors. He wants to blend in and thus become invisible in a wholly public space. The exceptions are heroic figures who tend to die on the field of battle.

The constant exposure of the body at war involves a total denial of its erotic character. Love of nation is to replace love of any particular body, including one's own. Sacrifice displaces pleasure as the source of the body's meaning. This is a world of bodies exposed in all of their vulnerability. So exposed, they are denied any mystery. This is the ground of the distinction between the combatant and the noncombatant: only the latter still has a private life within which he or she can cherish the mystery of the body.

I imagine life at the front is rather like life in the emergency room of a hospital: broken bodies entering with complete anonymity. Except for the exposed wound, the doctor knows nothing about the patient. That is what a person rich in memories and associations has become: invisible in his very visibility. The difference between the emergency room and the front is that at the front the distinction between doctor and patient disappears. Imagine an emergency-room doctor who constantly thought that at any moment he might switch places with the patient. Everyone, then, would live in an entirely visible world; everyone would be invisible in that world. This is the great anonymity of battlefield injury and death. From this, we try to recover after the war, when we carefully list the names of the fallen on the battlefield memorial. Granted again their identity, even the fallen return home.

My father's PTSD showed itself in this soldier's attitude toward his own body. In his imagination, he was not a naturalist but a soldier. He hid within his public display. If he thought that anyone was looking at him, he panicked. As I think about this, I realize that I have almost no photos of my father. There are entire decades with no photos at all. There was no posing for the camera in his life.

Invisibility went beyond staying out of sight. It also meant never having to give an account of himself to someone in authority. Going to a doctor was, in his mind, not very different from having to give such an account. The first thing a doctor does, after all, is ask for an account. My father saw a link between authority and death—a link that makes perfect sense on the battlefield.

He only started to let doctors into his life after he was overwhelmed by the weakness of his aging body. About the time he turned eighty, he nearly died of a slowing heart. He had taken to his bed, thinking this too would pass if only he could reach a state of absolute stillness. He would not let my mother call a doctor. She did so only after he lost consciousness, and only after I insisted. Within an hour of the call, he was having emergency surgery to implant a pacemaker. He had needed it for years. He was startled by the way in which this small device returned him to a forgotten strength. This brush with death was the start of a change. He would have to let some doctors into his world, even if it reminded him of his vulnerability.

His visible invisibility, his fear of doctors, and his rejection of care might seem surprising given that his actual role in the war was that of medic. The only story that I ever heard him tell about his experience as a medic described his performance of an emergency tracheotomy with a fountain pen. To this day, I cannot see a fountain pen without thinking of it jabbed into someone's neck. This story symbolized competence, even heroic performance, under the stress of battle. The unspoken point, hidden just beyond this saving act, was of the many soldiers who must have died while he was trying to save them.

A medic with Patton's army, he saw a lot of death and a lot of pain and suffering. He came to the wounded when they were racked with injury, missing limbs, or leaking intestines. For most of them, there was not much he could do, apart from providing morphine to relieve the pain. This was not yet the era of helicopters swooping in to take the wounded to field hospitals. The capacity to heal remained well behind the capacity to injure.

Like many other elderly veterans, he went to see Stephen Spielberg's *Saving Private Ryan*. He broke his silence about the War when he came out of the theater. Of the stomach-churning scenes on the beaches at D-Day—scenes of bodies dying with no romance or mystery, and with repeated cries of "medic"—he said simply, "It was like that." This was the sum total of his report on the pain of his war experience.

He spent more than a year of his life amidst this unbearable suffering and death. The lesson he took away was that there is nothing erotic about the body. Indeed, there is not even anything private about the body. The potential for injury pulled the naked body into visibility and visibility was just a short step from death. This was not like working in a hospital, where scenes of death are relieved by scenes of recovery, and in which one can go home to a private life at the end of the day. It was simply the grinding away of bodily suffering. Serving as a medic was a lesson less in life than in death. It was a lesson he could never forget.

Some thoughts are just unthinkable. They shatter us to the bone. For many people death is like this. We break out in a cold sweat; we strike out at the pillow; we scream into the empty room, "No, this cannot be." We do not accept for a moment Socrates's calm argument that it is foolish to fear that which we cannot know. We already know that which we cannot bear to know: we know that we will not be. As an adolescent, I would tell myself that I have nothing more to fear from the nonbeing after death than I had to fear of the nonbeing before my birth. Just as what happened before I arrived was a matter of indifference to me, so should I be indifferent to whatever might happen after I am gone. That thought never calmed the panic. It never made death an idea that I could truly think. My father too found death an unbearable thought. At war, however, the thought was forced upon him endlessly. By the time the war was done with him, he could not think of anything else.

PTSD works as a kind of obsession—an inability to get particular thoughts or images out of your mind. You become stuck on a memory. No matter that you know full well that you are not on the battlefield, your imagination will not let you feel yourself to be anywhere else. Think of the experience of the battlefield as containing a thousand elements of sight, sound, smell, feel, and taste. Someone with PTSD can find himself pulled back into that world when he experiences any one of those thousand elements. The experience of that element need not even be conscious. It might be a scent or a flickering image that disappears in an instant. It brings in its wake, however, the whole of the world to which it has been permanently linked in the imagination.

This capacity to react automatically to a scent of danger is surely a legacy of our deep evolutionary past. We do not want to have to reason a situation out each time it recurs; we want to be immediately alert to the dangers it might pose. We are, so to speak, on a hair trigger, when the threat is great enough. For those with PTSD, the hair trigger keeps being pulled. They are unable to escape, to turn their thoughts elsewhere. Life becomes a flight from this trick of memory—an unsuccessful flight because the triggers are too many, too common, and too unknown. My father's life was just such a flight.

We all know variations of this experience of the trick of memory: the smell of a Madeleine for Proust takes him back to his youth. A few notes of a song can take us back decades. Suddenly we feel that we are somewhere we have been before; we speak of déjà vu. Some unknown switch has gone off, pulling up an entire world of experience. If that world was one of comfort and happiness, we feel this as the warm glow of memory. If it was one of threat and fear, we feel it as a living hell.

If there are enough triggers to a particular memory, we will keep circling back to the same experience. We cannot get over it; we cannot move on. One wakes up thinking that this day will be different, but then the first sight of daylight triggers a memory of what it was like to make it through a fearful night. Suddenly, one finds oneself back in the war again. For my father, one trigger was any experience in which he felt others were looking at him. This might be a doctor, but it might be anyone who asserted authority.

This obsession shattered the possibility of his getting on with his life. Yet, I cannot help but think that in it there was also an affirmation of life. He was endlessly willing his own existence. The sleepless nights were a refusal to stop this willing. Imagining himself sleeping was only a small step removed from imaging himself dead. To relax into sleep requires a kind of faith that one will return in the morning. Was that not the original point of bedtime prayers? Perhaps, to relax into death requires a similar faith. My father had neither form of faith.

His strategy was to be eternally vigilant, watching his body for the moment when his soul might depart. He would drag it back by an act of will. He would not go to doctors because he feared their message that death would come and there was nothing he could do about it. His sitting still in the presence of an ailment was similarly an act of concentration of the will: he was willing his own being. That sitting still was the counterpoint to his absolute rage when some injustice broke in on his life.

Of course, he knew that none of this made any sense. He would never have told others that they should not see a doctor. He was a man of science. New age practices and beliefs had no attraction for him. He would never openly admit that he had stopped seeing doctors. If asked, he would offer an excuse—"There is nothing wrong with me." Or, he would agree that he must set up an appointment. He would never carry through. His reason was simply no match for his imagination. He discussed this with no one. Just as he lacked faith, he trusted no one. It was him against the world. We could no more drag him to the doctor than we could drag him to a therapist.

It took my father more than half a life to escape Patton's army. Even that was not enough. Behind his plan of hiding in plain sight was a certain formation of character—or to speak more technically—a certain pattern of memory construction. What had happened once on the European battlefield could happen again. He was prone to new obsessive memories. The trauma of war may have been his first obsession. It was not his last. He had PTSD as a repeatable condition, not as a single memory.

With my mother's confession, he was in the grip of a new obsession. Again, he lost control of his memory. He could think of nothing else. He was stuck. He could not move on, but neither did he think that he should move on. The world was always just as he saw it. There was only one truth to be seen. No matter that it was unbearable. He would rage before the unbearable fact.

There was a cruel irony in this new obsession. Not just because on the Chesapeake he had finally freed himself of the War, but also because this new image was at the opposite extreme from his prior obsession. In the first, he could see the body only as threatened by death. After my mother's confession, he could see her body only as an expression of the erotic. Both the 1960s and the 1940s had offered a cult of the body. The earlier cult celebrated the body as the object of patriotic sacrifice. The later cult took the body back from the state and celebrated it as the source of erotic pleasure. It insisted on life over death. Not surprisingly, this new cult of the body was linked to an anti-war movement: make love, not war. My father could not be at peace in war or love.

The working of memory is always mysterious. How exactly is a memory held? We imagine it as if there were some sort of filing cabinet in the brain, but that metaphor is not very helpful. Who exactly is doing the filing, and how does he remember where to look? It is hard enough to think about how we get from a set of chemical reactions in the brain to intelligent action in the present. It is unfathomable to think about the way in which intelligent thought can lay dormant in brain cells. I once asked a neuroscientist whether it was helpful to think of the brain as operating like a computer with many memory chips at its disposal. He responded that it was extremely unhelpful. For one thing, we put intelligence into the computer, just as we take it out. The analogy would be helpful only if we thought that computers could evolve on their own. They cannot, but intelligent life did.

Memory may be unfathomable, but it is the fundamental principle of the universe. Order comes from repetition; it comes from doing the same thing and thereby remaining the same. Without repetition, there would be no identity. We could not walk in the same river twice. This principle of repetition is present in the cell that replicates itself. It is present already in the configuration of the atom: an atom is of one kind or another. If cells or atoms were to forget, if they were to become random aggregates, all would be chaos. There would be nothing at all. When the Greeks thought about this, they said form must be imposed upon matter. Matter without form is the chaos of nonbeing. We would say that there must be laws if there is to be a universe. Think of Einstein's quip, "God does not play dice with the universe." The point is the same: a world requires sameness through time. This is how we experience memory. It makes it possible for each of us to be a self.

I am not surprised to read that when we press physics far enough we learn that the line between matter and energy dissolves. Memory is not a capacity added to the smallest bits of matter; it is all that there is. Without memory, everything would be "without form and void . . . darkness . . . upon the face of the deep." I think of the energy that constitutes the whole of our known—or knowable—universe as simply the force of memory. The black matter, which we suspect but do not know, is that which lacks memory.

Memory is what makes one out of many or something out of nothing. If we ask that most basic of questions, "Why is there something rather than nothing?," the answer is because there is memory. I like to think of human memory as simply the point at which this sameness through time becomes conscious of itself. It is the echo of all—the cosmos taking itself as its own object of thought. It is my mother's "I am" and my father's endless willing of himself coming at us from every direction. When we lose our memory, we lose ourselves. If we entirely lose our ability to re-member, we lose the world itself.

Memory is mysterious to us just because it is the first principle. We think we need to explain its derivation from other things—brains or souls—that are more basic. But nothing is more basic. We do not teach infants how to remember; we teach them because they can remember. For me, to think of gravity as the curvature of space-time is impossible. I think of gravity as a longing to return. It is a memory of our original togetherness before the Big Bang. Entropy, then, is a forgetting. These are the two great forces of the universe: memory and forgetting. They are the two great forces in each of us.

The greatest gravitational force of a human life is love. Plato de-scribed love as the longing to return to our original state in which lover and beloved were joined in just one body. Genesis tells us the same thing: man and wife become "one flesh." We live our lives in search of our lost other half, and when we find him or her we feel we have recovered that original unity of one flesh. In the end, we all lose this battle to recover our memory of an original unity. We forget who we are and we fall apart. This is what we fear in the death of a loved one: the rending apart of the truth of ourselves.

My parents really had become two in one; they were bound to each other for better and worse. The force of the binding energy between them can only be called love. But love is not a force that necessarily excludes hatred. Hatred does not rend the universe like death. It does not forget; rather, it pulls us toward the object of our hatred. In my father's final obsession, love and hatred could no longer be separated. Not for him, not for my mother, and not for me. Perhaps this was equally true of his first obsession. Did not his first experience of PTSD arise out of a different kind of love—love of the self? We find death unbearable because we love ourselves. Can you so love the self that you come to hate the world?

My father's prewar resentment was coupled to his postwar obsession. He was simultaneously in a moral crisis and an existential crisis. He de-manded justice and he wanted immortality. Unfortunately, neither was on offer. The consequence was the pattern of his life. He kept to himself; he was perpetually restless. He fantasized about moving to a Caribbean island. He took up sailing. He liked to read books about solo crossings of the oceans. To be alone on a vast ocean was his dream: an ideal of flight from everything and everyone.

He never made it to one of those solo crossings, but neither could he stay in one place. Immediately out of the army, he used the GI Bill to pursue graduate study in chemistry at MIT. It did not work out. He never spoke of what went wrong, but I cannot imagine how he could have tolerated the relationship of subordination a graduate student has to his professors. He did not know how to act toward anyone who might have served as a mentor. An academic mentor can be generous or demanding. My father would not have known how to respond to either. He did not know how to be anything but the center of his universe.

He fled from Boston to Chicago, where I was born. There, he fled from chemistry to law. He went to law school at night, while working in a laboratory during the day. I suspect that part of the attraction of night school was that it was a flight from parenting. He got his law degree and he moved from a laboratory to a law office. Again, it did not stick. We were in flight again, now to New Jersey where he worked for a large corporation. He lasted a bit longer there, constrained by his children's need to finish school. Yet, he was so eager to move on that he left before my sister finished her last year of high school. In flight again, he bought a small marina on the Chesapeake. At last, he would owe nothing to anyone. He still, however, had himself to deal with. And, then, there was my mother.

At the marina, his flight ended. He managed there for fifteen years—a record for him. He managed, however, in spite of himself. He was a very poor businessperson. Most of all, he had no sympathy for his customers. He thought they were acting unjustly, trying to take advantage of him. He brought to his business the moral outlook of a Soviet collective: everyone should do their share. He would be outraged if someone placed a bag of garbage on the ground near a trashcan that was full. The right response would have been to take action to correct the situation. Why put the burden on him? The list of injustices was endless: people failed to park in the right place, they played their radios too loud, they occupied too many picnic tables, and they were careless in tying up their boats. There were no written rules. The demands of justice, he thought, were obvious to everyone. Failing to meet his standard of what should be done, a customer could find himself evicted.

None of this had anything to do with paying for services. I never heard him complain about customers who did not pay. The issues were always moral: violations of his sense of justice. Nothing gave him more pleasure than kicking out a customer. In his small space by the water, the moral order of the universe had finally been made right. His family thought it better that he take out his resentments on his customers than on us. They, after all, had far less to lose.

His business survived because he could rely on my mother, who continued to have a steady income from her own work. Despite his dependence on her, the business was not a partnership. She had no interest in it. She might answer the phone occasionally, but that was the limit of her engagement. I never saw her in the office. I am not sure she even knew there was a shop. I never saw her on a dock except to get on their own boat.

On the Chesapeake, he found relief from his postwar obsession. I do not really know why or how. Perhaps it was the passage of time. Perhaps it was just the filling of his mind with the mundane details of a small business. Some boat always needed attention; some storm threatened; some dock was breaking down. Perhaps it was because he could pursue justice against his customers. Whatever the reason, life at the marina was as good as it ever got.

He implemented his own plan of justice, and he developed coping techniques that gave him some relief from memory. In his own way, he put himself on a therapeutic regime: the regime of hiding in plain sight. The way to avoid an obsession with death is to avoid having a body. You avoid having a body when you ignore the body. He would derive no pleasure from the body. It is no accident that the French call orgasm *le petit mort*. My father saw the link between sex and death, and he gave up on both. In his denial of death, he oddly anticipated death. Is that not the basis of every ascetic regime?

My psychoanalyst friend was surely right: there is a lot of Freud in this behavior. His regimes and rules were hysterical symptoms that cry out for interpretation. This book is my effort.

These were terms that my father had worked out for himself in his little kingdom on the Chesapeake. They were terms, however, upon which no one else had agreed to live. They were completely unacceptable to my mother. She was a tolerant, not an intolerant, person. She would never think of blaming anyone. She harbored no resentments. She did not want to drive people away, but to invite them in. She wanted to strike up a conversation. She longed for company. This was the least of it. She actually liked nature and beauty. She was not prepared to live in denial of her body. She did not see her body as threatening death. She surely had not given up on doctors. She wanted to be observed, for most of all she wanted to be loved. She wanted, in short, just those things that my father found impossible. Where she saw life, he saw death.

Looking back, it is hardly a surprise that she would find a lover. Why exactly not? If she was going to do any hiding, it was going to be the real thing. She had nothing to deny, only things not to tell. For her, not speaking of something—whatever it might be—must have been an immense challenge. I suspect, however, that keeping this secret gave her strength during those years in which my father lived out his fantasy of denial: the strength of knowing that his world was not hers, that there was some beauty in the world. He could loudly declare that his way was the truth. She did not have to argue with him because she secretly knew that there was another truth. Her affair put her in a position to judge him—a thought that he would not have been able to tolerate for an instant.

Had he learned of her secret life at the time, he would have left her. He would have followed the pattern of his entire life: flight. I do not know what would have become of him. Perhaps he would have ended up one of those homeless veterans that drift in and out of institutions. He certainly would not have returned to law; his small business would have failed without her. He would not have asked for help from his children. What would have been left? A person who denies everything can end up with nothing.

It is hard to come to grips with this situation in which they lived when they were younger than I am now. His life was one of denial; hers was one of deception. Remarkably, these double strategies successfully put off any crisis. Denial and deception are actually well matched. Since he was not prepared to confront his deepest fears, there was not much possibility of him seeing her truth. Denial actually invites deception. It begins with the small compromises of truth. No one, including my mother, wanted to call out my father on his intolerant and abusive behavior. No one wanted to lecture him on his own injustices. That complicity in denial led to the largest deception: her turning to someone else. My mother, whose constant chatter so often seemed indifferent to truth, must have found the entire world my father had constructed for himself an impossible lie. Deception fit easily into that world.

Truth, in my view, is a much-overrated virtue. Relationships are built on care before truth. Sometimes the truth is just too much. Surely, it was for my father. Still, there are limits to care, and some of those limits involve the truth. My mother cared for my father, but in the end, she just could not stand the fictions he so needed for himself. Because she cared, she continued to support him; she continued to indulge his phantasm that he was complete in himself. So the deception. This double life worked; it would have continued to work until the end of my mother's life had she not been overcome by the need to confess. Truth got the better of her in the end, with disastrous results. Maybe he had just exhausted her capacity for care.

A man who lives in denial does not press for the truth. My father never wondered about things beyond his vision. He did not want to know. In response, my mother simply chose to live outside of his line of sight. My father never knew and he never would have guessed. He had no curiosity, so he had no suspicion. He could not see the unhappiness of others even when it was all around him. He was not interested in the pain—or the pleasure—of others. He probably thought that he was putting truth over care, but of course he was blind. He was constantly averting his gaze. He knew that if he let his eyes wander, he would see only his own death. And that was a vision with which he could not live.

My mother knew, until she became so old that she forgot, that my father simply could not handle the truth of her affair. She knew instinctively that this would kill him. He would flee, but he had nowhere else to go. The shore of the Chesapeake was quite literally the edge of the world for him. The only remaining destination for his endless flight was over that edge and into insanity. When she did confess, he went right over that edge. Unfortunately, he tried to take her with him.

Up to the moment of the confession, the two deep pathologies of my father's emotional life had been kept more or less separate. First, there was the injustice of the world: he was always threatened with becoming the fuckee. Second, there was the frailty of the human condition: he was going to die. His anger at injustice was not quite the same as his rage at mortality, although they were at times as difficult for him to tell apart as they are for me looking back at all of this. I think of the latter as his nighttime activity, bringing on the cold sweats and insomnia. The former was his daytime preoccupation, leading to his intolerance of everyone. Both alienated him from others; both made him entirely ill at ease in the world. They fed off each other, but they were not identical.

Even if he had lived in a perfectly just world, he still would have carried the burden of mortality. Even if he were immortal, he still would have confronted an unjust world. One was the tantrum of a fatherless child, while the other was the scar of combat. True, he devised a common response to both: flight. When he could no longer flee, he was overwhelmed by both resentment and obsession.

Just as it became difficult to tell them apart, it was not possible to know which condition was more destructive. If he could have cured just one, I do not know which he would have chosen. Nor do I know what I would have advised. Would you choose justice over immortality or the other way around? Would you choose to live forever as a slave or would you choose freedom even if it meant death? The choice sounds like something out of a Greek myth. "Live free or die" is the motto of New Hampshire, but it was not written with the idea that immortality was an offer.

My father would not have been a happy man, even if he had never gone to war. Injustice would, in that case, have been the theme of his life. Conversely, even if he had been at home in a just world before the War, he still would have returned from the front with PTSD. The War taught him something deep about himself, even if he could not bear the knowledge: the body is a death sentence. For him, this was the great injustice that confirmed all of the others. That is where his two obsessions finally intersected: we are an immortal soul condemned to a mortal body. He may have been an evangelical atheist, but he struggled with the same problem that religion has always addressed: original sin.

I used to test my children's inclinations for immortality by asking them whether they would rather be alive in a box or dead in a box forever. Personally, I always found it a tough question to answer. I wondered whether a fertile imagination could keep me occupied literally forever in that box. I cannot quite imagine the moment at which I would decide that I was sufficiently bored to call it quits. Suicide is just not in my nature. I suspect, however, that I am not quite accepting the terms of the question. I harbor the hope that I will get out. This is like harboring the hope of rising from the dead. Indeed, my question is only the secular form of testing one's belief in resurrection. My father, a man with no religious sympathy whatsoever, always chose to be alive in the box. He did not worry that he would get bored. He knew, however, that this choice was not an option. No matter what, he would be dead in the box.

I have already described my father's reaction to my mother's confession. If he had believed in gods, he would most certainly have thought that they hated him. He was the new Oedipus, suffering for reasons known only to the gods. Like Oedipus, he had sought to escape his fate by fleeing to a distant place. Also like Oedipus, he nearly made it. Oedipus had lived out much of his life as a good king, father, and husband before he learned the truth that it had all been a lie. My father had finished his Chesapeake sojourn. He had created a little kingdom in which "Capt'n Sam" ruled according to his own odd vision of justice. Like Oedipus, his effort to escape his fate created the conditions for his own destruction.

My father too could not bear the truth of the confession, but neither could he flee from my mother. Instead of following Oedipus's course of blind flight, he sought vengeance. I heard his stunning cry for justice and saw his collapse as he recognized that it was too late. He was trapped. She had beaten him; he was the fuckee. Injustice had pursued him into the marital bed itself. Here was the final and complete proof of the metaphysical character of injustice.

His response was to torment her right up to the moment of her death. My father was not a subtle man. He wanted my mother to experience real defeat; he wanted her diminished to nothing at all. He wanted to rub her face in her sin. He wanted her hopeless and in pain.

His aggression was never a secret language between the two of them. It did not play out in signs and symbols that only the two of them knew. It was, instead, the verbal equivalent of unending physical torture. There is a reason that the international torture convention extends to "cruel, inhuman and degrading punishment." Those were just the areas of my father's expertise. He knew no limits on what he would say. He could not stop the stream of verbal invective that would pour forth at any moment. She would have to admit that she had committed an unforgivable sin against him. Every other possible meaning of the act was to be brutally negated as nothing more than her own sojourn in Sodom.

She would always end her acknowledgment with a "but I was lonely." For him, there could be no excuse. He would not hear of it and she must not speak it. An excuse suggests some reason, and there could be no reason apart from her desire to strike at him. Imagining my mother and her lover, he saw himself ridiculed, ignored, and cast away as nothing at all. Believing that he was the center of the world, he could not ask himself what was going on from her point of view. If he felt ridicule, then it followed absolutely that she had done this to ridicule him. He would make her suffer every bit of pain that he felt. Because his pain was endless, he set out to cause her endless pain.

My father may have served as medic in the War, but in his old age, he practiced the skills of the torturer. The torturer aims to turn every memory, every human connection, against the victim. If the victim loves his wife, let him hear the screams of pain inflicted on her. If he has faith in his comrades, let him believe that they have betrayed him. If he hopes for rescue, convince him that no one is coming for him. This was my father's strategy. Where my mother might have remembered pleasure, she would be allowed to see only pain. Where she remembered the embrace of another man, she was now to see only my father's wound. She was not to think that anyone or anything would save her from this endless pain. Her lover was dead. Her children would not challenge their father. Her friends would stop visiting. The world was shrinking to just the two of them: the torturer and his victim living together in the same cell.

In her own way, my mother joined the battle. She was not without her own skills of survival. She knew that he could never be free of her. She would come back at him with her own voice, "But I was lonely . . ." It is quite impossible to say who suffered more pain. They simply struck at each other ceaselessly until she lost the power to strike back and he was left alone.

While my mother could continue to engage him on the field of justice and injustice, there was nothing she could do when he fell into the pattern of his PTSD. Here, he was on his own, and there was nowhere to go but into the sinkhole of a memory he could not escape. That she was the source of this new traumatic stress gave her no special power to relieve it. She was like a German soldier who had aimed a gun at my father. The memory of the image did its own work, quite independently of what happened to that soldier or what he might feel today.

During the day, my father would seek vengeance for the injustice he had suffered. At night, he would lay awake stuck in an obsessive act of imagining my mother in bed with her lover. Torture might occupy his days, but it provided no relief from his nightly obsession. With nightfall, he moved from torturer to the tortured. Whatever relief he got from his imagined triumph over my mother during the day, disappeared when he faced himself at night.

His first trauma arose from the death and destruction of the human body in war. His second trauma was no less tied to the body. Now, however, it was sex, not death, that occupied his thoughts. What linked these two obsessions was absence. In each case, he was compelled to see his own absence. The image of the dead body said to his imagination: "You are not." Imagining my mother's affair, he heard the same message from her, "you are not."

Each of us knows there is a before and an after to our lives, just as we know there are countless places in which people live whole and complete lives without us. We make sense of our own lives by placing ourselves in this narrative stream of history and within an emotional geography that tells us where we belong. We form beliefs about history and space without noticing our own absence. We make predictions about the future, without questioning whose future it is. Similarly, we study the past without noting our own absence. Yet everyone has had the experience of being taken aback when reading of a Chinese city of millions of people of which one has never heard. It is a little like learning that there are intelligent beings on another planet. One feels one's own absence. Can there really be so much life without me? Whole schools of philosophy have answered this question skeptically. PTSD is hardly a philosophical school, but it lives with the same skepticism.

I rarely heard my father talk about the future. Nor did he speak much of the past, and, of course, close to nothing at all about the first twenty-five years of his life. He never began a conversation with "Remember when . . ." or with "One of these days, we will have to . . ." Even as he got old, he lived in the present. He had a similar relationship to space. Early on, he stopped traveling on vacations—but for the winter migration to Florida. He complained that travel was not worth the effort. He wanted to be in just one place: his own home. He had no curiosity about others because he could not imagine a life from which he was absent. He did not want to see what he was missing; he could not accept the idea that he was missing anything at all. What he saw was all that there was.

I am eerily thrilled to stand at a historic spot. I find an inexplicable pleasure in standing on the battleground at Gettysburg or visiting the rooms of Monticello. I imagine the Native Americans who traveled my woods and walked on the same rocks over which I now climb. At such moments, I catch a glimmer of the experience of the sacred. I understand why people make pilgrimages or how the ancients felt at Delphi. I harbor still a regret that I did not become an archaeologist, although I suspect that the professional attitude might have driven out my deep delight. Similarly, I am easily drawn into movies about the future or the past. I want to imagine what it will be like to live in the future; I want to see exactly what the buildings looked like, what the people wore, and how they went about their lives in the past. My father had none of this.

I think of my capacity to consider the whole of time, from the Big Bang to the cosmic crunch (or is it a cosmic diffusion?), as just what it means to be made "in the image of God." It is an unfathomable privilege to bring the whole of the world—all that has been or will be—into consciousness. Yet, it comes with a cost. I am filled with an uncontrollable sadness at the thought that our world is doomed, that history had a beginning and will indeed have an end. I find no consolation in the fact that the end is very far away. To think that there could be such consolation is to deny the privilege of having a mind that spans all of time and space. Perhaps this ontological sadness is a remnant—genetic or otherwise—of my father's fears of not being. Perhaps in time those neuroscientists at the VA hospital will suggest that I am a candidate for a pharmacological intervention to treat my own capacities for memory. No doubt, they will tell me that I suffer from thinking too much.

I hope not, for I am describing here the religious imagination. I could not convey my thoughts without invoking Genesis and the myth of man's creation. That cosmology has replaced eschatology is only a sign of the times. The impact of the thought of the end of the cosmos remains the same whether we explain that end through myth or physics. The same is true with respect to individual deaths. Understanding the causes of a disease does not make the death it brings easier for any of us, whether the death is our own or that of a loved one. My relationship to the universe is a kind of love: I mourn its certain demise. No amount of science can relieve the burden of that knowledge. I can laugh at my inclination toward imagining the end of our world, but if this is a comedy, it is also our deepest tragedy.

My father had no such imagination. For him, there was only one time and only one place. After the confession, his memory held him tightly in the time and place of my mother's affair. As far as he was concerned, that affair was all that existed. He could neither get back before the event nor find a future free of it. He could not take a God's-eye view of creation, spanning all of time and space, because he was stuck always at the point that marked his own transition from presence to absence, from being to not being. Not the end of the universe, but the end of himself filled his imagination. I imagine his mind racing feverishly trying to find the answer to the puzzle that has no answer: how to end up alive in the box. He lived quite literally the death of God.

We are held to the world not just by our own imaginations but also through our trust that others hold us in their thoughts. We exist most fully when our friends and loved ones organize their lives around us. We know, then, that we are a real presence in their lives. Without this network, the relationship of each of us to the physical world would be one of irredeemable loneliness. It would be as if one were living the life of the last man on earth. We find some comfort in the thought of the sorrow of loved ones at our own death. This is why we imagine dying surrounded by those whom we love. With this thought, painful as it is, we know that there is meaning to this world.

Because we exist not just in our own bodies but also in a network of social meanings, we can die two kinds of death. The body can give way or the social world can give way. We use the expression, "he was dead to society." The ancients understood this form of death when they offered exile in place of execution. Rather than kill himself, Oedipus exiles himself into the empty space between the social worlds of cities. We have lately rediscovered the effectiveness of this form of death when we "disappear" alleged terrorists into secret prisons. My question to my children about life in the box was a way of bringing out this second kind of death: to be alone in the box is to die to the social world. "Is that a life at all?" I would ask them. My father's first trauma forced him to imagine the death of the body; his second forced upon him the death of the social world. The latter was no less shattering than the first.

Imagining my mother's affair, my father saw his own nonbeing. He saw my mother speaking words of affirmation to her lover and words of denial to him. In my mother's incessant "I am," he heard her saying "you are not." Once this image was in his head, he could not get free of it. That is the nature of PTSD. Imagining his wife with her lover, he was screaming to himself "where am I?" He was not in that world, and so he was not at all. There is only one death of the body, but the soul can be killed many times. My father was suffering his second murder.

My mother's confession told my father that he was alone in an unjust world. It told him that he was a dying piece of flesh with no hope of redemption. In her confession, he heard words that confirmed his deepest belief that we are bound to this life until the moment that we die, and that is all there is to it. He was not going to get over this, because there was nowhere to go. Deep down, he believed she was right: There is no meaning to this life. On this point, there was no argument to make; there was only the bearing of an unbearable thought. Once it had entered his mind, it filled his vision. He was, like the prisoner on Death Row, a dead man walking.

He was Prometheus chained to the rock, having his liver pecked out by eagles. Every day he would wake up to find the eagle at him again. Can one live with the knowledge that tomorrow will be just more of the same? For that is what it means to be enthralled by an unalterable memory. The courage to let go of that memory is not very different from the courage to move forward in combat. Both require an act that simultaneously acknowledges the finitude of life and affirms the self in the face of death. We get the strength to make that affirmation from love. At that point, death becomes sacrifice. For my father, there was only the rock and the eagle.

It took my father fifty years to flee from the nightmare lesson of battle. If he had had another fifty years, it would have taken him that long to flee the nightmare of my mother's confession. As it turned out, he had very little time at all to mourn his own death. She not only appropriated his entire imagination, she literally took possession of all his time. For shortly after her confession, we learned that she had cancer.

Chapter Three

Death

My mother was never a particularly healthy person. She was always going off to see one doctor or another. They would diagnose conditions that were persistent, but not life-threatening. Her maladies were always at the edge of serious. Not enough to effect what she did, but just enough to be on the daily agenda. The term "auto-immune" was often used, but unlike other people I know with such problems, she was never on much of a special diet and she was never on steroids. It was from her that I first learned what it means to be lactose intolerant, but the only real evidence of this condition was the soy milk she used in her coffee and the occasional announcement that she had taken a pill, before eating a rich dessert. I was aware of all these health issues, but they never seemed anything about which to be terribly concerned. Approaching eighty, she still seemed to have her physical ailments under control. She certainly needed nothing from me.

She had an odd combination of confidence and skepticism when it came to her doctors. On the one hand, she extended to them the Jewish mother's customary awe of their profession. To her, each of these doctors was some mother's child. One had to respect that fact. Right up to the last weeks of her life, she was thrilled when a doctor showed up in her hospital room. That he was there on ordinary morning rounds would not have occurred to her. It was, for her, a visit. On the other hand, she never quite seemed to get the relief she sought from them. Because of this, she spent a lot of time looking for new and better doctors. Maybe she just enjoyed meeting with different doctors, just as she enjoyed meeting with new people wherever she went. Each appointment promised the thrill of a new encounter—with a doctor no less.

I do not know if the doctors killed her in the end, but my father certainly thought so. He believed that the doctors were so used to looking for the odd gastrointestinal symptoms of her autoimmune maladies that they missed the real problem: cancer of the spleen. It was only when she wandered into yet another new doctor's office that she actually had a physical exam by a doctor who was not looking for anything exotic. This doctor immediately noticed what no one else had thought to check: a much-enlarged spleen. Something was very wrong, and very obvious. Perhaps earlier detection would have helped. I doubt it would have saved her, but it might have given her some relief from the onslaught of serious symptoms in the year before the discovery.

That was a terrible year of decline. Her body just started to let her down. Not in the gentle way that happens with the progression of age, but as in the systematic collapse of what had been a well-tuned machine. She could not eat much; she always seemed to have a fever. She could not rally the strength for her old engagements. With the decline of her physical health, came a decline in her mental health. Her memory became worse and worse. She could not carry on a conversation without endless repetition. Worse, she could not be trusted to carry out the simple tasks of living on one's own or, in her case, with my father. No driving. No cooking. She might leave an open flame on the stove or put metal in the microwave. She could not organize herself well enough to clean up their condominium. She could do little more than sit and wait for visitors. She would still light up when someone came by to talk with her. She wanted to hear what was happening. Indeed, she wanted to hear it repeatedly, since she could not remember from one moment to the next. At each repetition, she was thrilled yet again.

Her rapid decline infuriated my father. He could not help but blame her for her condition. After all, he believed that he could will himself to health. He did not exactly expect her to follow his medical practices. He might avoid doctors, but—except for therapists—he was eager for my mother to see specialists. Still, he read the need as itself a sign of weakness. His universe was a moral order at its metaphysical core. Nothing in his world just happened. More precisely, it was all happening *to him* for a reason. However, he did not stand with Job's friends, who thought God must have a good reason for inflicting punishment. Rather, he thought my mother was punishing him for no *good* reason. He may have completely rejected God, but it seemed as if his universe was still full of demons.

Her physical decline was something she was doing to him. If so, she should be able to do something about it. He felt this instinctively, even if he could not say it aloud. He was still calculating the injustice in the universe. Her increasing dependence upon him was not just. That he should be taking care of the woman who had so sinned against him made no moral sense. Could he possibly combine rage and care? He did take up the tasks that she shed, but he could not do so without an undercurrent of resentment. His anger had not abated. It was not displaced by sympathy for her physical suffering. The anger had not even been deferred. At most, it was frustrated and redirected. It was always just below the surface and it would regularly explode.

He lived with the constant memory of her as the younger woman betraying him, but that memory was now his alone. It was beyond imagining for everyone else. The disjunction between her current physical frailty and this image of sexual betrayal was just too great. For several years after the confession, they had shared this memory and fought a constant struggle over its meaning. Now, he could not even share the memory with her. Perhaps she still had the deep memory, but she did not have enough of a short-term memory to carry on the battle. She could not follow a conversation of any length, any more than she could remember it once it was over. He could, however, still accuse her of many other failings, which he did not hesitate to do. If she failed to take her pills or failed to eat enough, she was doing this to him. She slept too much or she did not sleep enough. If she could not remember something, she was arguing with him. If she remembered something differently from him, then she was just wrong. If she did not see that, then she was obstinate. That she was simply very ill could never be reason enough. There were never any excuses in my father's world. His own behavior was not excused, but justified. Everyone else was simply failing.

I think there is something to my father's suspicion of medical negligence on the part of many of the doctors she saw. My mother, however, was not entirely without fault in creating this situation—just not in the way in which my father thought. It had nothing to do with him. Nor did it have anything to do with weakness of the will. My guess is she misled the doctors through her endless inclination to talk. She would come into the doctor's office with a long account of all that she felt was wrong. I can imagine her setting forth her symptoms, which would move on two continuums at once: from real to imaginary, and from serious to minor. She probably had trouble sorting these out. As she talked, even the most imaginary symptoms would come to seem real to her. Or, she might start her account with the least serious of her issues. Whatever she was talking about she absolutely believed, but she talked about whatever happened to enter her mind. As her memory and reason failed, the confusion of the true and the not-so-true—as well as of the serious and the minor—became worse.

If the doctor expressed an interest in one symptom, she would dutifully embellish it. She would forget everything else for the moment. It must have been very difficult for a doctor to know exactly where to look for the cause of the array of symptoms that she would describe. On top of that, she would have trouble staying on point. The description of one symptom would lead her to some free association of people or place. Suddenly instead of localizing a pain, she would be pursuing Jewish geography with the doctor. She never left a doctor's office without at least recounting the lives of her children and grandchildren. More than that, she did not leave without having learned from the doctor of his or her children and grandchildren. When she discovered that one of her cancer specialists knew me from long years of using the same gym, she was delighted. She reminded me of the connection each time I saw her. I am sure she reminded him as well. She was no doubt memorable to the doctors and nurses because of the human connections she made among people who are dedicated to abstracting the symptom from the person, the disease from the character. All the nurses, aides, and doctors I would run into at the hospital knew my mother. They always sent their greetings through me. Their concern was genuine. For a long time, they just could not figure out what was wrong with her.

Late in her life, I had some direct experience of this difficulty of genuine communication about her problems, although by this time admittedly her mind was not working all that well. I had taken her to the emergency room because of a fall that worried me. She had just gotten over some sort of systemic infection; she was barely eating; her blood pressure was dangerously low; and she had already had one major surgery. The list went on and on. I wheeled her in to see the triage nurse, who asked her what was wrong. To my amazement, my mother started her account of her health problems by saying that she was suffering from a heart murmur. It was true that she had a heart murmur. It was also true that she had had that condition her entire life and that it had no health consequences whatsoever. For some reason, this was the first thing that came to her mind and it was, accordingly, what she first offered as the source of her problems and her reason for coming to the emergency room. I thought it funny at the time, but it was characteristic of how she dealt with doctors. She wanted to chat, just as she would chat with anyone else who crossed her path. This conversation could begin anywhere. The point was not where it began, but where it ended—in a tangled web of connections. A doctor who knew nothing about her might have dutifully started investigating her heart problem, when the reason she was there was an injured hip.

Unsurprisingly, most doctors ended up confused. They could not tell what sort of an ailment was the cause of her symptoms; they could not even give a coherent account of all the symptoms. Her account would change from visit to visit as she confused one doctor with another. Inevitably, they had to wonder if at least some part of it was not psychological. No doubt some of it was. There was no denying that the stress of life with my father was taking a serious toll on her health. That, however, had nothing to do with the cancer in her spleen.

As she got older, her problems just got worse. She really did become sicker. But also, she had less and less capacity to present her symptoms coherently. It would have helped if my father had stepped in and tried to mediate between her and the doctors. That did not occur to him until she was literally incapable of acting on her own. He did not deal with doctors. He did not deal with illness and pain, or anything that would remind him of his own mortality. Years before, he had made this clear when he failed to deal with my appendicitis.

If the two of them had appeared together in the doctor's office, at any point before her final year, they would only have offered up their battle for display. He would have burst out at her, for he could not control his anger even when they were in public places. In fact, my father probably stayed away because he was afraid that my mother would mention their battle as a source of her troubles. He knew that somewhere in the course of her conversation with the doctor, she would set out her confession. How else would she have answered the question, "How are you?" Hearing the confession, the doctor would no doubt have started wondering if she needed a referral to a psychiatrist. Like the rest of us, he would not have known to whom to refer my father.

If I can imagine that this is the direction in which her conversation with her doctors would have gone, so could my father. Imagining this, he resented it. He absolutely rejected the idea of her talking about him with anybody at all. He knew that there could be no such talk without judgment. He had fled from any situation in which he might be judged. Nevertheless, here was my mother inviting just such judgments under cover of illness. In his view, he was not a medical problem; he was a victim of her injustice. If he had been at the doctor's office, he would have had to explain that however ill she might seem, he was the real victim. Sympathy should be for his suffering soul, not for her suffering body. Her suffering was some sort of cosmic justice for what she had done to him. Of course, she would have responded that she had been lonely, that she had not found what she needed from him. So it would have gone, just as it was repeated countless times before countless innocent third parties. If they had been children, someone would have called a time out. As it was, there was no escape short of dying.

There was another reason why I focused less on my mother's state of health than I should have. My attitude toward their health problems was established well before the moment of her confession. As they grew older, the person in poor health was my father, not my mother. My mother may have had a long list of odd symptoms, but she had had them for a very long time, and mostly they were not visible to me. That my mother was not well was routine, but it was not threatening. Whatever her condition was, it was being managed. She took her pill and ate dessert. My father, however, seemed to be in rapid decline as he approached eighty. He had never been in very good shape: always overweight, never exercising, never paying much attention to his diet, and, of course, never seeing doctors. His cholesterol was high and his heart was weak. He had been a smoker; I can still remember the cigars and then the pipe. He was depressed and he was turning away from the things he used to do. He had sold his business. He had little to fix or repair. For a while, he attended classes at the extension college, but he gave that up—they too were all idiots.

He seemed to be slowly shutting down. He would spend his days reading *The New Republic* or *The Atlantic*, venturing out little. Movement was becoming difficult for him because of problems with his joints and the problem with his heart. He tired easily; he climbed stairs only with great difficulty. To me, he seemed like a heart attack just waiting to happen. Then, he had the incident with his heart slowing almost to a standstill and the emergency implantation of the pacemaker. Standing in the hospital room with my mother after his surgery, I tried to speak to her about what she might do were he to die. She did not want to speak about it, but clearly it was on her mind. "Assisted living" was a phrase that suddenly starting appearing in my conversations with her. She was going to investigate assisted-living facilities.

It was not easy for me to come to the realization that all of this was backwards. My father was not so much shutting down as taking care of himself in his own odd way. This crisis with the pacemaker had been something of a turning point, because the fear of being near death—not an abstract idea of death—pushed him to the point where he started to accept the idea of seeing doctors. He had, after all, to get the pacemaker checked regularly. Unlike my mother, he had no trouble describing his symptoms. He could be clinically precise and demanding. Again, un-like my mother, his ailments seemed quite treatable. He started taking medications. He not only recovered, he got much stronger. While I was worrying about his health, hers had become extremely vulnerable.

Her real physical decline began a couple of years after the confession. It began deep within the years of ferocious struggle between the two of them. Even for me, it was hard to know exactly what was caused by physi-cal maladies and what was caused by psychological trauma. Many of her symptoms, I thought, were caused by the stress of my father's relentless attacks. I still think that was true. It is just that the proportion of the psychosomatic to the somatic shifted in favor of the latter over the course of a couple of years.

He was, I thought, killing her through his constant assault. He was pursuing her to the point at which the emotional became the physical. He was pushing her right over the edge. This was not an accident; it was not the by-product of some other problem that just happened to place extreme demands upon my mother. His response to her confession was murderous. She would defend herself, but the emotional and physical toll was tremendous. At times, she was barely hanging on. Of course, the same was true of him. It would have been more accurate to say that, locked in their embrace of love and hatred, they were both going right over the edge. They were clinging to each other as they fell—circlemen rolling over the cliff.

Once my aunt called me from Florida, where she and my uncle win-tered near my parents. They had just visited them at their condominium, where there had been an explosive scene of accusation and confession. They had known my father and experienced his emotional volatility for over fifty years, but they had never witnessed anything like this. She called to say that something had to be done, that my father was destroying my mother. I am sure she feared for her sister's physical safety. Not just a fear of physical attack. She may have thought that my father was driving my mother toward suicide; she must have seen the physical decline that had already set in. My father had been beside himself, ranting about her sexual misdeeds, throwing things at the walls, tearing up magazines and papers. He was not only in a blind rage; he was in a cold sweat. He was flailing at the edge of his own universe. He was doing the only thing he knew how to do, which was to throw himself with all his force against the entire world. He was screaming, "No! Not now, not ever!" There was nothing heroic in this, only panic, desperation, and rage.

No one could see this rage and not think he was in danger of a heart attack or complete mental collapse. Maybe that collapse had already occurred. He had become a force of blind destruction. What was uncertain was which of the them would be the first to simply give way before this force. Despite his deep fear of death, one might reasonably have thought he was actually acting on a death wish, driving himself to the point where he might indeed have a heart attack. He could not calm himself, and he would not accept help. His resentment drove him to the point where he thought of himself as a martyr, where his own death might seem the answer to an unjust God. His endless panic at the thought of his own death would be triggered by this inclination toward martyrdom, producing the uncontrolled outburst that my aunt and uncle witnessed. He could not live with his knowledge of betrayal; he could not imagine not living. This contradiction produced hysteria.

Despite the pain behind the rage, no one who witnessed his destructive temper could have any sympathy for him. Everyone's first thought was to try to save my mother. Something had to be done for her. I alone worried about both of them. His outbursts never served to relieve his internal pain. Rather, they only increased the trauma. That pain confirmed his sense that he was the victim. It was just more proof that he had always been a victim. He was raging not just at her, but at the whole calamitous universe that had brought him to this position. That my aunt and uncle were there made no difference, for his problem was not personal but cosmic. There was nothing to hide because there was nowhere to hide. If they could not see the world as he did, then they were idiots—an accusation he made against anyone who disagreed with him, which was virtually everyone. By the end of the evening, he was raging at them as well as at my mother. He drove them out of the house. He wanted never to see them again. The feeling must have been mutual.

My mother had tried to argue with him. Reasons were exactly what he did not want to hear. More rage; more flying objects. After my aunt and uncle fled, they called me. They were truly in a panic. My mother would not leave. My father would eventually storm out. But he had nowhere else to go and no place that would distract him from his obsessions. He did not know what it meant to blow off steam. He was not about to go for a walk and get it out of his system. He was not a drinker. He had no capacity either to forgive or to forget. He would quickly be back at it again.

After talking with my aunt, I called my father. I asked him, "Are you evil or sick?" I told him there were no other alternatives to explain what he was doing. For the first and only time in my life, I yelled at him. I told him this had to stop. I expressed no sympathy as he started screaming about what she had done to him. I tried to shock him out of his state of uncontrolled rage. I told him he needed treatment or he needed to move out. This relentless attack could not continue. If he could not live with her, I would help him move elsewhere. If he wanted to stay with her, I would help him find treatment. That he would take up either offer was about as likely as his taking up golf.

In his world, my accusation of evil made no sense. I had it backwards: he was the innocent victim. As for treatment, he screamed there was nothing wrong with him. He collapsed in tears. He became incoherent; he did not know what to do. What he was prepared to do was exactly nothing. He was where he believed he had to be. His entire life had led him to this place. When he looked at my mother, he saw only betrayal. If he looked at himself, he saw only death. We are, he thought, like flies to the gods, who kill us for their sport. In this world, there was only one honest response: to rage and rage, no matter what the cost.

So, it could be no surprise that my mother was getting sicker. Just being near them for an hour or two could make me physically ill. I felt as if I had to get out, to find some fresh air and some free space. I was secretly relieved when they would move to Florida for the winter. No one could have lived with my father without feeling sick much of the time. My mother was not eating well, she was not sleeping well, she was no longer going for walks on the beach, and, on top of all that, my father was making it increasingly difficult for her to pursue her favorite activity of simply chatting with neighbors and acquaintances. Surely, my aunt and uncle were not about to come back for a casual visit or a shared meal after their encounter with his rage. If not them, who? Who would cross the front line onto their battlefield? It was as if their condominium had one of those triangular danger signs hanging on the front door.

No doubt, many of my mother's symptoms were caused by the stress of the battle they were waging. Do we expect the victims of torture not to display physical symptoms of their psychological abuse? The doctors were not completely unaware of the stress, for increasingly I found her taking tranquilizers, antidepressants, and sleeping pills. None of these medications helped very much. None was commensurate with the roaring, overwhelming presence of my father. He was the vengeful god and one does not take a tranquilizer in the presence of the sacred, whether for good or evil. Neither did she flee. She stood her ground and continued the struggle. Like him, she was where she had to be. They had long ago made the choice for each other. Neither could imagine a life without the other, despite the endless pain that this life was producing. They were like a country in a civil war. Death and destruction were their lot; there was not some other country to which they could move simply because their own had become violently destructive.

In this competition of pain, it remained unclear who was suffering more. For my father, there was simply no relief imaginable. Yelling and throwing things could not make the universe right. At best, it could achieve a balance of pain between him and my mother. Her defeat would never actually relieve his pain. My mother, however, never felt guilt for her sexual transgression. She never yielded to him. She always had her reasons. Unlike my father, my mother could imagine an end to all of this. She kept her romantic vision of the two of them settling into the last stages of life. However, she had no idea how to get there. Getting to peace had been the point of her confession. She had no plan B, once her first plan brought down the heavens.

While the unrelenting struggle moved up and down the East Coast, age itself was taking its toll on my mother. However much grief and pain my father caused her, she really did have a problem that had nothing to do with her mental state: it was in her spleen, not in her mind. One does not cure cancer with more powerful tranquilizers. Once her cancer was identified, the medical professionals could organize themselves in a useful way. They knew how to get her strong enough to sustain the surgery, how to perform the operation, and how to bring her through recovery. She seemed to do just fine, weathering major surgery late in her seventies. The doctors reassured her, and us, that this sort of cancer is usually self-contained and that she should fully recover. This was yet another mistake, for within the year what had been lymphoma of the spleen had become lymphoma of the blood. From that, there was no recovery.

After the surgery, she was quickly back to her old self, talking to all who would come by her hospital room. Perhaps it was the forced separation from my father at the hospital—a time out—as much as the surgery itself that helped her regain some strength of mind and body. Whatever it was, she was better than she had been for several years. She quickly knew all about her various doctors. Even more important for her, she had found one resident who was handsome, Jewish, and, as far as she could tell, unattached. She could not resist the opportunity. From her hospital bed, she was plotting to get him and my oldest daughter together. Whether the doctor was interested or not, I have no idea. He probably faced this issue often, if his patients included a number of elderly Jewish grandmothers. That my daughter was not interested did not really matter: there was Jewish geography to be made.

I imagine that patients, particularly those in the cancer wing, are usually a depressing group. Not my mother. The hospital was, for her, a relief from home. She could overlook the drip in her arm or the dressing on her abdomen and happily chat with whoever came by. She spoke easily with everybody—from the nurses' aides and the orderlies, to the medical students and professors. They all liked her and tried to spend some time with her. She was always interested in their families and especially interested in talking about her own family. Not just her granddaughter, but also all of the extended relations were to be reviewed. Sure enough, usually some connections would be found with whomever she was chatting. I would show up and she would tell me that the brother-in-law of one of the nurse's aides ran a store in the town in Rhode Island where we have a summer home. How, I wondered, could she possibly have found this out?

During this first hospital stay, my father adopted the pattern that he would follow over the next year, as my mother repeatedly returned to the hospital. He would be there in her room through the middle of the day. He would not arrive early, and he would not stay late. All of his motions seemed to slow down. He took his time coming and going. Still, he had nowhere else to go during the day. He organized his time around coming to the hospital, for the only place he knew to be was with my mother. I was often struck by how he was taking care of himself through all of this. He did not come early because he saw no reason to disturb his morning routine. He went home early because he had an evening routine as well. If he had been asked about his schedule, he would have said there was nothing more for him to do at the hospital. There was no way for him to be useful, so why hurry or why stay late?

When he thought about being useful, "comforting" was not a word that would have entered his mind. I do not think he knew how to provide reassurance. He surely had no capacity to show care. This had always been true. When I was about twelve, I was sent to the hospital with double pneumonia. I remember my father walking into my hospital room that evening and announcing, "How did you end up here?" There was a vague sense of accusation in his statement. It must, somehow, have been my fault. That was more or less his attitude toward my mother, "How did you end up here?" By that, he meant, "Why is this happening to me?" or more directly, "Why are you doing this to me?" He could not see the world other than through his own suffering. That did not mean that he was not attached to her. He was so attached to her that he literally could not imagine being anywhere else. So he came, but he did not stay for long.

My father did want to be useful, but for him that meant doing something. I imagine he was always ready to perform that emergency tracheotomy with a fountain pen. At the hospital, however, there was nothing that needed his doing. He really had no idea what to do with himself in her room. He could make phone calls to relatives to let them know how my mother was doing. This, however, did not take very long. He was never one to chat on the phone. More often than not, he was simply aimless. He could find nothing to do, nothing to make himself useful. He got bored.

He would have a leisurely breakfast; he would take care of whatever chores he had written down on the small notepad he kept by the phone. He would arrive mid-morning. He learned quickly how to take advantage of the valet parking so he never had to walk far or wait long. Coming late meant that he missed most of the doctors' visits, which were generally early in the morning. In her room, he established his own corner, where he kept a few magazines and a comfortable chair. He would do the *New York Times* crossword puzzle. Toward the end of the afternoon, he would announce that there was nothing more that he could do for her, so he might as well go home. Since he had done nothing all day, this conclud-ing remark meant merely that he had reached the limit of his patience. Maybe it just meant he was hungry. Looking back at this, I see that he was already preparing for life alone. He was easing himself into his future.

He had no trust in the doctors and he generally avoided talking to them. He did not try to run interference for her. Indeed, they both seemed a bit confused as to which doctors and nurses were in charge of what. He was hardly the doting husband. He was just a mass of frustration—a tense presence in a corner of the room. Eventually, he might go for a walk around the floor. He rarely spoke to anyone else on these walks. He never offered a sympathetic ear or support for the many patients around him. If anything, he would criticize them and their guests for not behaving as he thought they should. Too much noise, too many people in the rooms, too many children in the halls. Nurses failing to do anything about the offensive behavior.

I rarely found the two of them in conversation. They were not pass-ing their time speaking of their mutual past or planning their common future. When he did speak to her, it was usually to criticize. That was what he did when he got frustrated. It was also how he imagined being useful. He did not explicitly continue their unresolved battle. In the hospital, he observed a kind of forced cease-fire. His anger remained unrelenting, but even he knew enough not to explode in rage in a hospital room. He could not exactly start throwing things around. He could not even make a lot of noise. He redirected his anger toward more immediate complaints. She was not sitting right, she was not eating right, or she was not answering right. Nothing she did was ever right. Everything was, indeed, deeply wrong, but for this kind of wrong, he lacked words. She was, unsurpris-ingly, relieved when he would announce that it was time for him to go home. Then, she could do what she most enjoyed: chat with her visitors.

She liked it when I would show up after he had left. I too found it easier to visit without him there. She wanted to talk; he was incapable of talking about what was actually going on. With him, I would try to talk politics just to keep his mind busy. With her, I would talk about the doc-tors or about what she had discovered about various people in the course of her day. She would ask about her grandchildren. I would answer, and then she would ask again. I did not mind. She would share her plots for getting the handsome doctor together with my daughter. Often, however, she wanted to talk about my father. She would try to be sympathetic, telling me that all of this was very hard on him. She worried about him and wanted me to make sure that everything was going all right at their home. There was never any anger or blame.

Despite the difficulties of getting through it all, her initial round of surgery was good for both of them. It was the time out that they both needed. It was as if the doctors absolutely prohibited any mention of the struggle. They both knew that it was still there, that nothing had really changed. Nevertheless, a truce had been declared—not by them, but by the peacekeepers around them. Both came out stronger, but that meant only that they were ready to begin their struggle anew once my mother got home. Perhaps they were even eager to return to their old life. Surely, he was. I drove her home from the hospital. He carefully helped her from the car to the house. He felt useful. I wondered how long until the artillery would start up again.

Not long; a few weeks at most. Those weeks were good. For one thing, both my parents thought she was cured. Not only cured of the cancer, but also cured of the range of symptoms and maladies that were themselves caused by her cancerous spleen. They had reason to be optimistic, thinking the source of her long spell of bad health was gone. With confidence came a kind of strength. However, good health was not the cure for what ailed them, because illness was not the source of the problem. My father was really doing no more than waiting; he was repositioning himself during the lull in the fighting. This had been only a cease-fire, not a peace treaty.

Because it was summer, they moved their battle outdoors. This was a tactical advantage for my mother. She was much better off sitting with her friends and neighbors by the pool. He would have to rage in public, which had to be more difficult than carrying on the battle indoors. Not that he was incapable of it, but even he felt the new levels of sympathy for my mother, who, after all, had just returned from the hospital. He spent more time sulking. Instead of screaming at her, he had to employ more subtle forms of attack. He would belittle her in public; he would accuse her of incompetence over the most trivial of matters. She could not make lunch properly; she could not organize herself even to get to the pool; and she could not get the right items at the grocery store. She, however, had a supportive audience for her own defense. She knew how to use it. She would invite people to sit with her. He knew what they must think of him.

They were locked again in their struggle of rage and confession, even as it took a slightly more subdued form. The hospital stay had changed nothing. Instead, it had made all of this possible once again. It had been like a visit to a field hospital, exactly the sort of place that inhabited my father's deep memory.

So the summer passed. I was out of the country for much of it. I did not have to be there to know what was going on. By the time I returned, my mother's health had again started to fade. The same symptoms were back: infection, lack of appetite, weakness, loss of memory. With no spleen, how could this be happening? Again, there were all the old questions. Was it the stress of living with my father or had something new gone wrong? Was it actually something new or was it a recurrence of the cancer?

This time, her mind was even more deeply affected. She started confusing time and people. She could not remember where anybody was. If the deepest pattern of her memory was Jewish geography, the disturbance had now reached deep into whom she was. Worst of all, she started confusing who was alive and who was dead. At one point, she asked me if I was still in touch with my old boss. I told her, "Not since he died." My father thought this hilarious, since he had died some ten years earlier. My mother laughed as well, but the truth was that she was no longer registering death as a permanent event. The dead were all still living in her mind and that was good enough. When she did have to confront the death of a friend—for example, at a memorial service—she would feel unremitting grief. It was as if the idea of loss was just too much for her, so after a little while she would dismiss the thought from her memory. She would be sobbing for a lost friend at one moment and in the next forget what it was that was so disturbing to her.

Shrinking into her own mind, lost with only an unreliable memory, she was losing the war with my father by default. Her loss, however, was not his victory. He had not won; she was simply giving up the battle. He still wanted from her that single confession that she had never given and could no longer give. He still desperately wanted to hear her say that it had never happened, that it was all a mistake. He got nothing. She simply faded out of the fight as the fall approached. I do not know if she even remembered any longer what it was that she had confessed. Or maybe it was just the opposite. Maybe she was living securely with that memory, but no longer felt any need to confess. Confession, after all, makes no sense once the pattern of time going forward has been broken. Her confession had always been about the hope that accompanies every free act. Now, she was losing both hope and freedom.

She was disappearing before my eyes. She seemed content with the fading of the struggle. She literally did not know what was going on. Given what had been going on, I thought this offered some relief. She still liked to chat with everyone and anyone, but increasingly she could not remember the course of the conversation or to whom she was talking. This is the point at which the young find it very difficult to be with the old. They do not understand why they have to keep repeating themselves. They get nowhere and are anxious to move on. What is the point of reporting on all the adventures and triumphs of your life, if that report is followed by the same question, "What have you been doing?" They do not understand that it is their presence, not their words, that is important. The old are beyond being impressed with life's adventures, new as they seem to the young. What they want is the reassurance of care. The visit itself is what matters. This fact of presence is what registered for my mother even as she asked the same questions again and again. Most of us are not very good at offering ourselves to the old. There was a limit to how often I could ask my children to visit their grandmother. There was a limit to how much even I could stand this. My father was well past the limit.

By early fall, we knew that the cancer was back. No longer localized, she had a full-blown case of lymphoma. She was now too weak for ordinary chemotherapy, but there was some new treatment of designer drugs that specifically targeted the cancer cells. It too was administered by drip. I never really understood the difference between this and chemo, except she was judged strong enough to survive this form of treatment. My father would take her to the hospital for a weekly treatment and it seemed to go well. He had a specific task that made him feel useful: get her to the hospital. That he could do. Once again, the doctors brought her back from near death. There was, however, no real recovery of strength this time. There was no thought that she was over this. Only a sense that somehow she had been granted an extension of time.

Late in the fall, I had to go on a trip for a week to give some lectures out west. I went by their condominium to say goodbye. I found my mother in what had become her normal position: huddled in a corner of the couch, barely occupying any space. My father was much as he had been at the hospital. Frustrated, not knowing what to do with himself. Now, however, they were no longer living a time out; this had become the routine of their lives. He was still redirecting his anger into criticism of my mother, only now there was a sense of desperation in his caustic comments. It was as if he were saying, "It has come to this? Where is the fight? Can't you even die right?"

My mother really did not have the resources to confront her situation. Her long battle with my father and then her battle with cancer had simply used up whatever strength she had. The two battles had merged into one. Life was a fight for presence, first in the confession, then in the hospital, and now at home. At moments when she could still think clearly, she expressed concern about being a good patient. She told me that she would do whatever the doctors asked of her; she would put herself in their hands. She said this as a concession of defeat. Everything was out of her hands. She had become passive. She wanted to trust the doctors, hoping that they could do again what they had done only a few months before with the surgery and her rapid recovery. But she was now in uncharted territory, and the doctors had no clue how to bring her back.

My father was forced to take care of her at home, but that gave him less relief than I thought it might. There was just not enough to do. He was efficient. He would get her up and park her on the couch. He would try to force her to eat, but she would decline almost everything. He would insist; she would pick at her food. He would try to get her outside for a short walk, but it was usually beyond her strength. Perhaps her decline triggered memories of his time as a medic. He was again face-to-face with the dying, and again he simply could not deal with it. His rage might have been quieting but his angst, his trembling before death, just filled the place of rage.

The last thing I said to them before I left on my trip was "Stay out of the hospital until I get back." I meant it humorously—an expression of hope for them and for me. Within twenty-four hours of my arrival in Colorado, I got a call from my father. They were at the hospital. My mother had some sort of new infection. The doctors could not locate the source. She was rapidly losing her strength. Her heartbeat was fading. They needed to have her there to administer massive amounts of antibiotics and to try to figure out what was wrong. The next day, he called back to say that they were giving her a pacemaker. Without that, she was too weak even for the drug treatment. I remembered that it had not been so long since he had been the patient receiving the pacemaker.

It worked well for him. I hoped it would for her. Indeed it did. I thought these things should be standard issue for the elderly.

I saw them a week later at my brother's wedding in Boston. It was very important to my mother that she be there. The pacemaker made it possible. Without it, she might never have left the hospital. Mostly she sat and looked happy. People came by to talk to her. She said she was fine. She beamed as every mother should at the wedding of a child, even though this was my brother's third. For her, it was no less important than the first. Perhaps she no longer remembered the earlier ones.

She had her arm in a sling to protect the stitches where the pacemaker had been inserted. She could not remember why the sling was there or how to use it. She found the sling annoying and would just forget that it was there. Her arm kept slipping out. My father was focused on this, constantly telling her not to move her arm. To no avail, except to increase his own frustration. I wondered why it mattered. He needed something to do, something that would make him useful. Or was it that he needed to locate a point of opposition? Her failures as a patient served both purposes.

The most remarkable aspect of the marriage ceremony was my father's participation. My brother had asked him to speak about "the secret of a long marriage." I am sure he was just trying to be kind. The irony of his request was not on his mind, only the idea of a celebration across generations. Personally, my father would have been the last person I would have asked to speak to this subject. The secret of a long marriage for him was fear and trembling, flight and rage. It involved hiding in plain sight and acts of random evil. It traveled the fine line between love and evil, of care and injury. The secrets of his marriage were indeed very secret. If they were to be spoken at all, the right place was certainly not at a wedding.

My father slowly mounted to the podium. Looking at my mother, he started to speak of the need for love, patience, and forgiveness. I was stunned. It was as if he had been reflecting back over the last few years. Was he asking her forgiveness? Had her approaching death finally shocked him into humility? Perhaps he was publicly chastising himself for his failures. For a moment, he showed that he knew more than he had ever spoken. He knew that he was possessed, that there was something deeply wrong with how he had lived, and that he had been unable to escape his fate. Now, he could at least stand back and condemn that life. Love, he said, was the only way out and the only way forward. Only for a moment, however, did he hold on to this thought. Just as sudden as this moment of revelation had been, there was a turn in his talk.

He went from the need for love to the need for "enlightened despotism"—a term that was still popular when he was in school. He said now that every marriage needs to be clear on who is in charge. Someone has to make the final decisions. The important thing is to make sure that the decisions are enlightened. There was his old devil: reason. He was still appealing to reason in an unreasonable world. Having confessed his love, he was now defending himself and reminding my mother—and the rest of us—that he was in charge. He deserved to be in charge because he was the smartest one around. His was the power to decide. He was condemning her not just for being unreasonable, but also for having made a decision without him. He could not let loose his sense that she had wronged him. I doubt my mother heard this part of his talk. For her, it was enough that he had said the word "love." I would guess this was the first time he had uttered the word in fifty years. I suspect it was also the last.

How to explain this? Was it that the words of love were only a show? Everyone knows that at a wedding one must speak of love. One toasts the newlyweds by invoking "long love." Was he just starting out as he thought he must? Could he be looking at my mother and offering his own confession? Was there a plea for forgiveness in this or was it only the banality of a toast? Was he overwhelmed by the moment? Was he remembering their own wedding and all the hopes he must have had then? Was his heart moved by seeing my mother beaming with happiness for my brother? Had he let death into his life at this point? If that was it, did he see at last that, indeed, there is only one way forward—the same way that my mother had seen in the romantic vision that had brought her to the confession? All of these were there, but none of these thoughts was enough. He could not sustain the moment. He did not break down in grief. Instead, he fell into the old pattern. Not love, but justice. Not equal parts of a single whole, but authority. Not death, but life at any cost. He turned his gaze away from love and from death. He could not bear to see exactly where he stood.

One should never be critical of how someone else deals with the presence of the dying and the fact of death. Certainly for my father, for whom the very idea of mortality was more than he could endure, sitting in the cancer ward was a test as difficult as running a marathon for others. I fear heights and will not go near the edge of a cliff. Sitting in the room for him was the equivalent of forcing me to spend hours on a cliff. I had to respect his turn toward the care of himself, much as I might have preferred that he turn toward care of my mother. I knew exactly the impulse he was following. I too wanted to escape the hospital unnoticed and get back to the ordinary successes and disappointments of family and work. I wanted the phone to stop ringing, because I lived in fear of what I might learn when I picked it up. Always the news was bad; always there was a new demand. The tension of waiting was overwhelming, crowding out everything else in my life. If I could barely stand the hospital, I was certainly in no position to criticize him.

He knew he was on very dangerous ground, and he was proceeding with great caution. His natural reaction was flight. To overcome that reaction, he acted in measured, small steps. If this is what it took to get him through the awfulness of it all, then so be it. As in the rest of his life, it was not that he did not care for my mother; it was just that the problems of his own life overwhelmed him. He had spent decades contesting the fact of his own mortality. He had lived in denial of his own body. Entering the hospital—the cancer ward no less—was like crossing the river Hades. Sure, he lived to retell the tale, but deep inside he knew that he was bound to cross again, and this time he would not return. The dying may be exploring an unknown land but we all know that we are destined to become equally familiar with it. This thought forces itself upon anyone who visits the hospital. It must have forced itself upon my father. Only someone who did not know him at all could have expected him to do much better.

In fiction, illness and death bring people together. We read stories and see films all the time on this theme: only with the threat of loss do we realize the truth of love. The care of the dying spouse, child, partner, or parent is an affirmation of love. The deathbed scene itself is a moment of extreme tenderness. More than that, it is a moment of self-definition, as the dying and the living realize they are bound together by a love that is greater than the separation of death itself. We want to confront death in the warm embrace of those whom we love. I mean this quite literally: we want to meet death in the arms of the beloved. When words fail, we think the physical touch can remain.

These representations of death defeated by love express our deepest hopes. This was so for my mother, whose confession was based on just such hopes. She thought that by confronting the end of their lives together, they would realize how they had been and remained bound to each other. My father knew as well that this was the plotline their lives were supposed to follow. He expressed that knowledge when he stood at the podium of my brother's wedding and started to speak. But knowing it did not make it so. This was a plot he could not follow. He could not let himself get that close to death; he could not imagine relief from the injustice he felt. Her death was unfair because he was not yet done with his rage. How could he rage at someone who could no longer offer any resistance? But what then was the alternative? To embrace her meant to embrace death, and that he could not do.

To help me to understand my father during this period of my mother's repeated hospitalizations and failing treatments, I thought about another encounter with illness and death of a few years earlier. Sally was a very close friend of Catherine's. They had worked together for ten years, spending much of their time together and becoming a part of each other's lives. Sally was in and out of our house and had been a large figure for our children for their entire lives. A high point of their year was the visit to Sally's house, a couple of days before Christmas, where they would all make Christmas cookies. Sally was young and she was unattached to family. Her parents lived in California, where she had grown up. Without family on the East Coast, she was much loved by a close circle of friends, including Catherine.

When Sally was diagnosed with incurable brain cancer, her friends took turns staying with her. Sally, they thought, should never be alone. They took this quite literally, making sure there was somebody with her every night. This continued for many months. Personally, I found being with Sally extremely difficult, for I was overwhelmed with thoughts of mortality that could not be spoken. I felt as if I were betraying her to have such thoughts. As a friend, even a somewhat more distant friend, I failed completely. I felt immense sorrow for Sally, but could not express it to her, nor really to anyone else. My sorrow, however, paled compared to Catherine's. She, however, had the strength to take up Sally's life as part of her own. The burden on her was tremendous, and tremendously destructive, but still she faced it. I turned away, trying to carry on the daily routines of our family. I told myself I did it for my children or for my students. I moved forward even when deep inside I knew that nothing would be the same as it had been. I certainly do not have the moral authority to criticize my father's care for himself in the presence of death.

It takes extraordinary commitment not just to bear the death of a loved one, but also to bear it with her. I do not mean the occasional visit to the dying. Nor do I mean the professional relationship to the dying achieved by the doctors and nurses. I mean literally to be there and to attend to death just as the person suffering is experiencing that death. I could not do it. One cannot do this out of a sense of obligation. It requires love. I liked Sally, but I did not love her. Love makes it possible to take up the burden of death, but it does not make that burden any easier.

For Catherine, losing Sally was losing a part of herself. To our family, this loss was as difficult as that of losing Sally. Actions done out of love may be necessary but they are not just. What was happening to Catherine was terribly unjust. Taking care of Sally destroyed Catherine's professional life, for that was something they had shared. Worse, she entered into a profound depression that took some years to overcome. Of herself, she said, "I became stuck." She lost interest and motivation, withdrawing from her old life. All of this was particularly hard on my youngest daughter. She needed a house filled with presence, warmth, and care. Ours often seemed to be filled with silent pain and suffering. But what else could be done in the face of the infinite demand that death makes upon love. It was too much to bear, but it had to be done.

I found the moral complexity of this situation profoundly difficult to understand, much less to negotiate. I resented the destruction that Sally's death was causing to my loved ones. In this, I was no different from my father, who so resented my mother's illness. It was indeed happening to him, as much as to her. Sally's death too had happened to all of us. Anger at this was just as important as sympathy for all the suffering. No less than my father, I could not fail to be angry at the injustice of the world. Anger at the injustice, however, was only half of the right response. I also knew Catherine was doing absolutely the right thing. It was a necessity of love. It was a claim upon her that had nothing to do with me or with our children. I knew I had to accept it and support it, even as I hated it. Could I combine my hatred for the injustice of the situation and still extend care to the patient and love to my wife?

I worked hard at holding on to both ends of the moral situation. It was important, in my mind, to absolutely hate the situation; it was equally important to be clear in my support for Catherine. It was a matter of moral integrity for me to rebel against the situation and condemn it for what it was: the kind of cosmic injustice with which my father was so familiar. I also had to hold on absolutely to the demands of love. I do not doubt that part of Catherine's depression arose from my own failings. At times, I am sure the hatred of the injustice seemed more evident than the love. Justice seems easy to calculate. We think we are on solid ground when we see that we are not being treated rightly. Love has no measure. It may not even have a voice. It can be an exercise in acceptance: to accept that which is beyond accepting.

Sometimes life presents you with tragedy. One of the sources of tragedy is the conflict between love and justice. We know this conflict most often in our relationship to our children. That a child of mine acts unjustly does not undermine my love. Justice is not a condition of love. However, love does not relieve the injustice. Because we love our children, we want them to be just. With children, we hope we can help them to achieve both: a life of justice and of love. Sometimes, however, injustice is not a correctable failing. It is, as it became for my father, metaphysical. Sally's death too was a metaphysical injustice. What it did to our family was a part of this injustice. Love was powerless to make it better, but still there had to be love.

The problem is deeper than the place of justice in love. The truth is that we cannot be happy without justice. The child who acts unjustly, no less than the child who suffers injustice, is loved, but she is a burden on the heart. We are not indifferent; we care deeply and we worry endlessly. Because love and justice run on different paths, there is no necessary connection between love and happiness. This was my mother's mistake, thinking that love alone could bring happiness. Love can just as easily take us to the greatest pain. For most of us, it will do so eventually. If it does not, it is only because, either fortunately or unfortunately, we die too soon. Love does not make the pain any less; it does not make the injustice of the situation any less. Christianity promised redemption for injustice through love, yet still it postponed the happiness until some future date. In this life, we may wait forever.

To hold on to both my love of Catherine and my hatred of the situation often required more than I could find in myself. To hold on to both love and justice was completely beyond the capacity of my father. He knew injustice. I am sure he knew love. In the middle of it all, however, he was simply overwhelmed. In his mind, he was always the victim. The gods themselves were against him. He did not find in his love for my mother the resources to deal with his own pain. Without that, he could not deal with her pain. He did not know how to be anything but the center of his own world. If he was not at the center, then it was as if he did not exist. This was no less true as he sat in the hospital. He was so used to fleeing from his problems that he did not know what to do when flight was no longer an option.

I do not have the strength to recount the last months of my mother's life in any detail. It was a modern death. A colleague once told me that today we die "a little bit at a time." My mother had been dying bit by bit for a year. At the end, however, the bits and pieces of loss came in rapid succession. The cancer came back and overwhelmed the possibility of treatment. She was back in the hospital but no one knew what to do. They would do tests, because that gave everyone a sense that they were still making progress—or at least that progress was possible. The tests, however, showed that everything was wrong. Systems began to fail more quickly than anyone could repair them. She would seem stable when I left her in the evening, but when I returned in the morning, she would have lost some other function. One night it would be a seizure; the next, severe mental disorientation. She would not know where she was or what was going on. Another night it would be her heart. The worst was when she had a stroke and lost the ability to speak. I can barely imagine the horror of this for her. Doctors still made plans for speech therapy, but it had become clear where this was going to end.

My father, through this time, was bipolar, just like at the wedding. One moment, he would be overwhelmed by grief and the next moment he would be criticizing her. He could not handle his grief, so he would turn to anger. At those moments, he seemed to think that if he could just get her to do the right thing—to take the pills or eat her lunch—she would recover. No one, however, could think this for long. Something would happen, the doctors and nurses would rush in, and he would be pushed aside. Then, it was back to grief. They would get her stabilized, and he would return to his criticisms. Even now, he was not prepared for her death. I could never decide whether his suffering was about justice or about love. It was just like at the wedding.

Love was just too difficult for him to hold on to, so he would turn to justice. He was being ripped apart by her illness, but his reaction, as it had been to adversity throughout his life, was a mixture of anger and flight. Just when I would begin to feel sympathy for him, he would turn on my mother. I would not turn on him, but only away from him. Her hospital room was not a scene of mutual support. We were each on our own to deal with the loss. Perhaps we are a family in which no one knows how to give or receive comfort. Like my father, I most wanted to be helpful. Like him, I could find little to do.

The end, when it came, came quickly. One morning I arrived to find her in intensive care with a breathing tube down her throat. She could still try to write, but I could not make out the weak scrawl. She knew what was happening. There was nothing of acceptance in her eyes or her movements. There was only panic. Clearly, at this point, her mind was working just fine. There was, however, nothing that she could do. Her will could not make her body work any longer. This lasted only a couple of days before yet more functions were lost. Doctors must make a judgment of how much of this a family can tolerate. They removed the tube and set all the machines at "comfort." The next day she was taken to the hospice. She was rarely conscious. Her last words to me and to Catherine were spoken with the greatest of effort: they were of love. She died early in the morning a few days later. No one was with her.

We often hear that in the modern age death has retreated into a nonpublic, professional space. We die under professional care, out of the view of others. We compare our lack of familiarity with death with an earlier age in which death easily inhabited the household. As long as people lived in extended families, death was always a presence. Not so anymore: dying is not a part of our world. The elderly live in a different world from the young, for the elderly most certainly continue to occupy a world very familiar with death.

This account of a world split in two between the young and the dying misses the real situation, which is not a division but a continuum. Friends start dying at a remarkably young age. We never seem to be more than several steps removed from the dying of someone we know. First, it is accidents and drugs. To me, college seemed full of rumors of the death of people with whom I went to high school. Next, it is cancer. Sometimes, illness strikes directly within the small circle of family and friends—as with Sally. More often, we hear of business associates, of friends of friends, or relatives of colleagues, who are struggling with a mortal illness. Then, we pass into that age in which it is parents. At that point—middle age—we enter an unending cascade of death. At least, it seems unending until you come to a point at which you realize that your parents' generation is gone. There is, at that point, a brief lull, and then you wake up one day to discover that your generation is next in line. We are then at the hardest point of all, watching friends and loved ones of an entire lifetime disappear. This is unbearably painful, but it is also the point with which the young have the least sympathy. We are back to the beginning, with the young living in a different world.

The hospice was invented as a response to the two-world view. It is to be a space for reconnection with family and friends after the isolating character of a hospital stay. Its values are community and care, not efficiency and treatment. Professional knowledge steps back, while the patient is returned to the love of family. Death is to shed its alien modern form and become again what it was traditionally—an inevitable part of life. Passing on is meant in the double sense of passing on life to new generations as well as passing on to death. It is, however, a good deal easier to express this ideal than to live it. At least in my mother's case, the distinction between hospice and hospital was not very great. The move to the hospice simply made final what had already happened in the hospital: she had moved to a stage beyond recovery and even beyond communication.

There was very little to share with her anymore for she was fading out of life extremely quickly. We knew she would die within a few days. Well before that, however, she slipped out of consciousness. There were no final stories to share; no coming to terms with a life that had spanned continents and decades. The end was so near that Catherine and I did indeed wonder whether we should subject our children to this. Is the sight of death important to the memory of a grandmother? We fall easily into thinking that we should protect our children from death. At that point, the idea of the hospice fails. It is not a place for grandchildren.

This was the first time I witnessed death up close. Actually, the best expression would be to say that this was the first time I was within touching distance of death. I had not been there at the end of Sally's life, which had occurred in the very same hospice. I found what I suspect virtually everyone finds: I recoiled from the touch. I had little more capacity to deal with death itself than did my father. The difference was I was never drafted. During the war, he had experienced death directly and without end. It overwhelmed him and set the pattern of his life. Most of the rest of us do not come so close to death until we find ourselves in the intensive care unit of the hospital, tending to the failing health of a loved one. The hospice was as close as I have come to an environment of death. Even there, however, I always knew my car was in the parking lot and that Catherine was waiting for me at home. I knew as well that it would be over in a few days, and that I would remain for now firmly on the side of the living.

It is not that I found the hospice to be an uncaring place. Just the opposite. Still, I did find it an extremely difficult place in which to extend my own care once my mother entered the final stage of her life. Not because the family was displaced by the machinery of life support as in the hospital room, but because the dying still hold something of their traditional character as a source of pollution. We really do not want to be too close to the dying. We fear the physical touch, when that is all that remains. The touch stripped of the promise of language turns out to be a most difficult moment. Maybe this was exceptionally true in my mother's case, since for her it had always been talk or die.

Before the modern age, people believed that death itself—not the illness that brought on death—was a dangerous pollutant. Contact had to be followed by rituals of ablution. In some places, the dead were handled by a special caste with whom ordinary people would have only minimal contact. We are not so far away from these beliefs. We continue to fear the touch of the dying; we rely on a special caste to deal with the dead. Modernity has not made our fear any less powerful. The science of health gave us the hospital; the science of sociology gave us the hospice. The problem of death, however, is not one that science can cure. At best, science can put off death. It cannot help us to accept it into our lives.

The hospice operates in a world stripped of the rituals that once eased the contact between the dying and the living. It relies on love alone—love unstructured by custom or tradition. I have no doubt that we moderns love the dying as much as our predecessors did, but I am not at all sure that love is enough. We need more than a space and an occasion for love. We need the faith that comes only with a practice of love; we need traditional ritual. This is more than the hospice had to offer.

Many years ago—before the invention of the hospice—when my father's mother was in the hospital nearing the end of her life, a doctor cousin of mine told me that we, the family, all needed to embrace her. The physical comfort of the human touch was what she needed most, for she was beyond the point at which she could respond to voice alone. He had seen enough of death to know this much. He went on to observe, however, that this family, into which he had married, did not easily embrace each other. He was prescribing touch as a difficult therapy to an overly cerebral family. I think now that he was right in his prescription, but probably wrong in his view of the extraordinary character of our family. It was not just my family; virtually everyone retreats from contact with the dying.

Not just the touch but also the presence of the dying is difficult for us. There is more than a technical reason that dying rarely occurs at home anymore. When it does, it is usually because it comes suddenly, before the ambulance can arrive. I know there is a new movement of home hospice care. I have nothing but admiration for those who can do this, but I do not believe it will ever become a major presence. Whatever our capacities for love, they are no longer up to the problem of death. Perhaps they never were, which is why death was always separated off from daily life by rituals and castes.

At the hospice, I did see people who were able to move in and out of this world of the dying. I do not mean the professionals—the doctors, nurses, orderlies, and clergymen. They could do their jobs more or less well; I certainly appreciated those who performed well. I remember the matter-of-fact way in which a doctor informed me, within minutes of ar-riving at the hospice, that my mother "would die here within a few days." She offered a clinical appraisal of how that death would come about. She assured me it would not be painful, that "comfort" would be adminis-tered. She was neither cruel nor kind. She was matter-of-fact, profes-sional. She gave this talk several times each day. I never saw her again. My mother was no longer a problem for doctors. She was passed on to the lower levels of the healthcare system. That, after all, was the whole point: care not treatment.

I can understand how one gets used to work in the hospice as a pro-fessional task. Even undertakers manage their jobs. Not the professionals, but the volunteers truly impressed me. After all, if one wants to volunteer in the community, there are many places at which one can lend a hand. Who chooses the hospice? Personally, I would head for the daycare center—a place to which I have longed to return ever since my own children moved on to elementary school. If one does not like small children, then what about the soup kitchen or the reading program at the library? There is so much life to affirm in these acts of care. But the hospice? How does one overcome the instinctual feeling of pollution among the dying? Surely, reason alone is not enough to bring us through this experience of dying and death. Is it an act of will that allows one still to see the person in the dying body? Or is it an expression of faith? The volunteers shared this practice of care with the ministers and rabbis who would make their way daily among the rooms.

Even my father was not indifferent to the care offered by a minister. I could not believe it when I heard him respond to an offer of prayer—Christian prayer, no less—with less than an offended rejection. There was none of his usual cynicism. Nowhere his evangelical atheism. Instead, I heard resignation when he told the minister to do "whatever you think best." Perhaps he was just completely disoriented in this environment of death. He too had no idea what role he was to play at the hospice. In this strange world, he did not want to violate what he suspected were the implicit rituals for the dying. The minister's offer was part of the total package on offer.

We are all in and out so quickly. Not just the dead, but also the living. We do not receive any instruction book telling us how to play this game of dying. When we come in, the doctor tells us to renounce all hope. At the hospital, hope is always cultivated. Entry into the hospice means leaving hope outside. We have little time to adjust from hope to hopelessness, before it is over. Still, to see my father fail to react angrily to the offer of prayer was a shock. He had spent a lifetime condemning as idiots those who find any relief in religious faith. They say there are no atheists in a foxhole. Maybe the same is true at the hospice.

Strikingly, many of the volunteers were elderly. Why are they not put off by the thought of their own deaths that the hospice must certainly trigger? They manage to live in both the world of the living and that of the dying. They come back from the latter sanctified, not polluted. I concluded that I was looking at the sturdy remnants of an age of faith. So much better to have them than to leave the dying entirely to the professionals and the distraught family members who do not know what to do.

For the most part, however, there remains a caste of those who handle the dead. Indeed, the caste is stronger than ever. They are invisible to the rest of us most of the time. We stumble into their world only at moment of death itself. We find that we have no place in it. We want to get out as quickly as possible. They know what they are doing; we do not. We yield up everything to them and play the minor roles to which they assign us. Often, not much more than sitting quietly and signing papers.

There was one particular role assigned to me for which I was not prepared. Shortly after my mother died, Catherine and I found ourselves alone at the hospice. Suddenly, the nurses were asking us whether we wanted to spend some time with my mother's body. This was not a question that I had expected. When I tried to decline, I quickly realized that the question was only rhetorical. This was how my father must have felt with the minister. Family members, I inferred, are expected to attend the body. We were there, the task was ours, and the time was now. When I protested that the setting did not seem right—the private viewing room was not available—I found myself speaking to the head nurse who explained their customary practices. If I was not prepared to participate, then counseling was available for me.

I knew when to retreat, and soon enough we found ourselves with my mother's body. I did not know how to handle this time. Do we need this presence to experience the deepest moment of grief? Or, is the presence of the body supposed to mitigate grief? I am sure I did not need this to locate my grief, and I am quite sure it offered no mitigation. I had a sense that I was participating in a ritual, but I was never told of the steps I was to take. There was no priest to show us the way forward. This whole process was a point on some sort of checklist for the professionals: "opportunity for family viewing." They knew they had to bring the body in and take it away after the appropriate amount of time. They had no views about what happened in between. This is what happens when ritual breaks loose from faith.

The hospice is nonsectarian, so they made a space for ritual without themselves offering any specific ritual. They were saying, "Now is your time to do whatever it is that you—meaning your people—do with the dead." Except that no one had passed on any such rituals to me. I have no "people." I have only Catherine. Together, we felt the unbearable silence of bodily presence without life.

Thinking about this event now, I realize that it was not just an opportunity for sectarian ritual, but had become its own sort of ritual within the hospice. This was how the hospice staff offered their own professional respects to those who had just died. This is why I was given no choice. They were acting, in part, on the necessities of their own practices. It would have felt offensive to them to move the body directly to the technical processing facility in the basement. There must be a pause, a moment of respect for the fact of the loss of a life. How quickly can we imagine the person disappearing from the body? We need to make some space for the departure of the soul, even if we have no faith that there is a soul. Without this ritual, we could not answer why we keep the dying alive at all. Why not just a practice of euthanasia once the dying are without hope? We must believe in the person, even when all we see is the failing body. The death of the body cannot itself be the moment that ends the relationship. It cannot bear that weight. To move too quickly to disposal would tell us that we were simply waiting, not loving, at the end of life.

I found myself, accordingly, participating in a rite of passage. Unable to rely on any tradition, this postmodern ritual had been stripped bare of any content except for the movement of the body from one room to another and the gathering together of the living before the dead. But what were we to do then? We did not even know whether we were to touch the dead. Prayer? To whom or for what? We were left with memory. We did feel it as a final moment of departure. To feel an absence is to feel the ache of memory, of a world that has been lost and cannot be regained. This psychological state of pain now substitutes for the traditional faith in reunion hereafter. If ritual was invented to ease pain, today we have ritual as an occasion for pain.

Whatever it meant or failed to mean to us, this act of being with the body gave the professionals permission to dispose of the dead. I do not mean this technically or legally. Symbolically, at the end of this ritual, the body was given over to them. There must be some denouement, some mark of a mission accomplished, if the hospice is to affirm its own sense of itself. I had encountered death and was forced to take up the ritual role on offer. Probably, this is the way it has always been. The modernity of the hospice is only its external face. Inside, we find caste and ritual; we find priests and saints. How could we not? For death remains what it has always been: a part of our world that we desperately feel does not belong here.

The postmodern character of the ritual of the hospice hardly means it is failing in its institutional mission. The question is: "Compared to what?" It may well be that the ambition to make possible an intimate community in the comforting environment of the hospice is beyond reach. Nevertheless, for those patients who are conscious of their approaching death, the hospice is surely a better place to be than the hospital. For those of us who are bound to the dying, the hospice offers the scriptless rite of passage from life to death and back to life. We act as witnesses to loss. What is beyond the capacity of any institution is what we most want: to make possible a love that can transcend death. For that, we are on our own.

If I did not know what to do and could barely endure the presence of death at the hospice, it was well beyond my father's capacities. He would have made a good primitive, for he felt even more strongly than I the pollution of the dying body. Death was a presence that he had been fleeing all his life. He had long ago turned away from the body—his own and others—because they all bore the scent of death. He could not help but see the skull beneath the flesh. Before my mother's confession, I have no memory of him ever embracing me. I did not think there was anything odd in that; it had nothing to do with me. I cannot remember him making physical contact with anyone. Surely not my mother. He was literally incapable of the physical touch, just as my cousin had noticed many years earlier. This did not change with my mother's illness; it did not change in her final days. He was overwhelmed by the nearness of death in her unconscious body.

Part of him, I am sure, wanted to embrace her and reassure her. Once the doctors were at the end of their protocols of treatment, however, he had no reassurance to give. He knew how to help, but not to comfort. While my mother was beyond understanding the meaning of her final ambulance ride, my father was not. It traversed the river Styx. As far as he was concerned, the hospice was on the far side of that river, and he wanted his visit to be brief. He had no beliefs, no faith, with which to comfort her—or himself. What was there to do, beyond wait for the end? The gathering of family was of no help to him. A community of faith could not just materialize out of nowhere. Each of us was there to suffer our own grief, not to form a community of the grieving.

And then there was so much that could not be said. We all knew of the raging struggle my parents had pursued over the last few years. We all knew of his violent rage, his outbursts of uncontrolled anger, his efforts at public humiliation, and his verbal abuse. Perhaps he thought that if no one mentioned it, then it was as if it had never happened. But it had indeed. We could not make the world other than it was. What he wanted from this small group of family, had he been able to admit it to himself, was not on offer. No one would charge him with anything in the midst of all this grief, but no one was about to forgive him either. He again wanted to be invisible.

My father was never able to resolve the conflict between his love of my mother and his sense of the profound injustice she had done to him. Without reconciliation, he had raged at the universe. In the hospice, each of us now faced a kind of mirror image of that problem: our love for him was inextricably linked with our sense of the injustice he had wrought. To be with my mother was to confront the problem of love and death; to be with my father was to confront that of love and evil. Emotionally, things do not get much more complicated than this.

The step from love to death is so short as to be no step at all. We do not first learn of it at the hospice. The deeper the love, the more familiar we are with death. I learned this when I had my first child. I would sit by my daughter's bed and read to her at night. She did not want me to leave after I had turned off the light. I would stay with her until she fell asleep, which in her case could be a good while. I relished the opportunity to be alone with her and with my thoughts. I found, however, that my thoughts inevitably turned to death. I would look at her and think that this is the person who will bury me. I could feel my death in the peace of that room. I imagined the scene, although in my imagination I was always somehow alive in the box. I saw her throw the first shovel of dirt on to the coffin. I knew this was to be. The only question was: How long?

What a startling thought this was. It is not a thought with which one can be at ease. It is not something that one gets used to. To stare at this image of love and death each night, as I tended to do, is a modern form of Saint Ignatius's spiritual exercises. I was challenging myself to find the strength to deal with this truth. I told myself that this is what love means, when you tear away all of the daily preoccupations of life. It is joy at birth that becomes, without even a moment in between, grief at death. The grief moves in multiple directions. I found grief in the thought that I am doing this to my daughter. She will have to bear the burden that is my death. The better a parent I am, the larger this burden will be. No one, however, is this selfless. This concern alone would not make it a spiritual exercise. There is also the grief of missing her, of knowing I will not be there to see the whole of her life. This is the aching feeling of absence from one's own world. Then there is the existential angst of death itself: the shattering thought of not being, of knowing the world without being of that world. It is no surprise that, back in the age of faith, each day ended with a prayer to God and a hope that we would still be here in the morning. Each of my days ended with the felt absence of such a prayer. Now, as I think back to those moments, I realize I was enacting my own form of prayer.

There is no love that is not deeply tainted with this sense of death. Once, when my children were still little, a friend, who had no children of her own, was visiting us. She offered to take my place in reading a bedtime story to my daughter. She felt the pleasure of it, musing about the sheer delight it must be to share in a child's innocent world. I loved that world with its constant discoveries and simple joys. I still ache for its loss, long after my children have grown up. I told my friend, then, what she had not imagined: "I cannot look at my children without seeing my own death." She was quite shocked to hear me say this. She simply could not comprehend it. I was reminded of an old saying, "Never trust a philosopher who has not had children." There are a surprisingly lot of them: Plato, Aristotle, Hobbes, Locke, Kant, and Mill—to name only the most famous. I learned half of what I know from my children. The other half I learned from my parents. From both, I learned of love and death.

My father was not about to take up the spiritual exercises I had pre-scribed for myself. He must have seen his own death in his children, but from this, he fled. He did not embrace the sense of tragedy that touches all love. The physical touch of love always seemed to him to bear the cold touch of death. He had about him nothing at all of the martyr, no idea of self-sacrifice. This, after all, was exactly the point of my soulful, nightly exercise. If death is the destiny of love, then my father's answer was to turn away.

To be so locked inside himself might have seemed an odd thing for such an emotional man. Not so strange, however, when one considers how he got to where he was. He was, in some deep sense, still fighting the War. There, he experienced that combination of physical rage at the enemy and fear of death that characterized him for the rest of his life. The body at war is a tool for the destruction of others, as well as of the self; it is not a source of comfort. His body was then, and it remained, the vehicle of his rage and the source of his vulnerability. These habits of a lifetime did not give way in the presence of my mother's dying body. Indeed, her death only confirmed for him what he had always known: the flesh is nothing but the site of death. The final years of her life taught him that even the object of his love could become the enemy. There was nothing new in this: how many times did God threaten to destroy the Israelites for the injustice they had done to him?

In myth, the real puzzle is neither the existence of the immortal gods nor that of the deathless soul of man. Mythical man is confident of his deathless quality. Life in the body is what we do not understand. We know our place is with the gods, for we know ourselves as ideas that have neither beginning nor end. Plato captures this in his myth of life before birth, when we lived among the immortal Forms—the perfect ideas of all that enters into the world of becoming. A modern version of this would be to think of the deathless quality of mathematics or of the physical laws of the universe. When we think a mathematical formula, there is nothing of our own bodily finitude before us. The thought and the object of thought become identical: there is no separation between grasping an equation and the equation itself. We are, at that moment, at one with Plato's Ideas. Before there is anything in particular, there are the timeless laws that govern all that can ever be. When we contemplate these laws, we know that we are not entirely of this world of changing things. To explain how the deathless soul entered a dying body, we invent myths. Today, we do not have the myths, but neither do we have an explanation.

The puzzle we must confront is death. Deep inside, each of us believes death is not a part of our lives. We belong with the eternal universe, not with this wasting body. It was just this idea that gave Socrates confidence in the face of his death sentence. Why worry about death, he asked, for either the soul returns to its rightful state of immortality or death signifies nothing at all. There is much to hope for, and nothing to fear. Philosophy itself, he tells us, is best thought of as a practice of dying, for if our ambition is to know the Forms, then we must act as if we are dead to the comings and goings of ordinary affairs. Knowledge and truth, being and beauty, all coincide once we escape the burden of the body.

Today, this Platonic ideal is quite counterintuitive. Philosophers, no less than everyone else, want to practice living, not dying. We stand not with Socrates, but with Woody Allen, who, when asked about the kind of immortality he wanted, responded that he wanted the kind in which he lives forever in his apartment. Plato's offer of immortality had nothing of the personal about it. After all, there is no difference between your contemplation of a mathematical equation and my contemplation of the same equation.

I do not really know how many of the classical Greeks could accept Socrates's teachings about immortality. I suspect that many of them longed for Woody Allen's kind of immortality. They longed for this when they sat with their children, reciting—if not reading—the stories that would ease them into sleep. Christianity spoke to them because it understood that we face the future not with the philosopher's confidence in our own immortality, but with the parent's grief before the knowledge of death. Christ promises not a return to our natural state of knowledge among the deathless forms, but bodily resurrection. We can hope to be together again and, this time, forever.

Christianity offered personal redemption, and we in the West gladly accepted the offer. We no longer needed to shed the body as a burden on free thought. Indeed, reason was no longer the highest value. It had been deposed by love. Unlike knowledge, love is always of the body. The puzzle of the relation of the body to love, and of both to death, is at the heart of the mystery of Christ. The promise is that we will be born again in the body of Christ. To get there, we must first have died to our own bodies in and through his sacrifice. This is the movement of love. We must overcome death through love. No one can understand this, but generations have found comfort in the double promise of love and life: "He who believes in me shall never die."

Who can believe this today?

Our secular age has not returned to the premodern confidence in immortality. Instead, we are bound to the body and, without faith, we are bound to death. For the most part, we live as Christians wanting bodily immortality, but without belief. We want the promise, but we have lost the faith that made it possible. Without philosophy or faith, the question is whether we can live with the knowledge of our own death. The lesson of my father's life is that we cannot.

Chapter Four

Faith

There is a state park near my home. Near a pleasant picnic area, a small stream joins a river that runs through the park. Just up from where the stream meets the river, there is a makeshift bridge. There, we released my mother's ashes. They quickly ran down the stream to the river and from there, away to the sea. About a dozen of us had gathered. Strikingly, no friends. Only relatives. Of course, friends would have been elderly and it was not an easy spot to reach. The decision had been my father's. We were all deferring to him. He said he wanted the minimum. What he really wanted was no trouble.

Why this deference? His grief was no more than our own; his claim, no more than our own. I felt as if I were participating in some deeply embedded replay of Freud's Oedipal myth: the child contests the body of the mother but loses to the father. The dominant male suppresses the son, who can only become a real man when he murders his father. I certainly did not have the strength for that. Nor did my siblings. There was only one person with murder in his heart in our family. So here we were, still playing our familial roles of father and child. Old and broken as he was, he still ruled. It made me wonder about all of those scenes in books and films in which a wizened old man occupies the seat of power despite the strength of his youthful sons. Usually, however, those scenes are set somewhere in southern Europe. They remind me of the mafia, not modernity. We were following the same pattern, but we had nothing of the mafia about us.

It was not sympathy, but was it only habit or fear? Was it just a habit of deference or did we still fear his rage? We all knew what he was capable of or at least that of which he had been capable. I certainly feared that he could easily move from grief to anger. Listening to words of loving memorialization about my mother, I easily imagined him muttering that it was all "nonsense." Would he rise up and put everyone down? Would he insist on describing the world as he saw it? Would he claim that he was the victim and deserved our sympathy, for she had betrayed him? Would he attack my aunt and uncle, driving them away again? Would he simply storm away in a rage?

Even if we made it through the memorial service in peace, we all feared what would come next. He was returning to an empty house, and none of us knew how he would take this. His life, after all, had been bound to my mother's. Even in his rage, he had been inseparable from her. What exactly would he do without her to love and to hate? He was not about to join the bridge club. His behavior over the past few years had alienated everyone they knew. I was not about to offer him the guest room in our house. Neither were my siblings. Exactly whose responsibility was he now?

It would be too generous to ourselves to say that either sympathy for his loss or worry about his future made us reluctant to assert ourselves. Around my father, everyone was always anxious to get back to their own homes. There was just too much threat of explosive energy in him. We could not help but be nervous near him. None of us wanted the burden of this man; none of us was prepared to take on the kind of battle my mother had fought with him. None of us thought he would change now. That he would find peace and friendship was quite inconceivable. Love was out of the question. What we did not know was exactly how his rage would show itself in my mother's absence. We feared we would become the objects of that rage.

My father spoke vaguely of having some sort of larger memorial service in the future, when he would feel up to it. He and my mother had been to a fair number of these services lately, and my mother usually came home quite moved. She would have liked nothing more than the thought of all her friends coming together to talk about her. Talking about her connection to their lives would quite literally carry on the tradition to which she had devoted her life. I did not believe that my father would ever feel up to it. Indeed, it never happened. How could he want to bring together all her friends and acquaintances to talk about what her life had been like over the last few years? She had confessed widely; they all knew what had been going on. My aunt and uncle were not the only ones who had expressed concern to me. They were not the only ones driven out of the house or leaving in fear for my mother. Most had witnessed some part of the struggle, which had hardly been hidden behind drawn curtains. It must have been the subject of many conversations outside of my parents' hearing. He knew that many of my mother's friends had offered her counsel, and that it was always the same: "You must leave that man." A memorial gathering, he would have thought, would not be to remember her, but to accuse him.

Nor could he could imagine himself standing up before such a group and offering his own memorial to her. What memories would come to his mind? Their long life together, or her betrayal? Would he speak out of love or hatred? I would not trust him, and I do not think he trusted himself. If he started to speak of his long love, he might not be able to control his imagination as it quickly pulled him back to his obsession with her affair. He would end with the question he could neither answer nor abandon, "How could she do this to me?" Silence was safer, he thought, and I had to agree. I thought of his failed words at the wedding: love always gave way to justice in his mind.

Even without the memorial service, the same problem of memory and response could surface in every expression of sympathy from friends and acquaintances. His answer to this possibility was the same as his response to every other difficulty in his life: flight. Flight no longer meant moving on; it meant withdrawal. He would simply have nothing to do with anybody who might challenge him. This was the test he would pose to all who approached him: would they accept him without blame? A few polite words acknowledging his loss were acceptable, but nothing more. No invitations were accepted to sit together and think back over her life. Those who suggested that they did not accept these terms were crossed out of his address book. No one was to intrude into his inner life. He did not want to have such a conversation even with his children. Occasionally, I would hear him say, "Mom would have liked this," when we were at some event together. I never heard him say, "Remember when." There were to be no shared memories.

To any outside observer, it might seem shocking that he felt no guilt at my mother's death. He may have worried that others would think him guilty of acting terribly, but his own moral responsibility was simply not something about which he thought. He was always the victim, always innocent. If he thought about those last years of struggle at all, he asked himself whether he could forgive her. Whatever he might have thought about this, the truth was that he could not. That she had died did not fundamentally change his obsession with the image of her in the arms of another. He could not shake this image from his memory. He did not see the face of an old woman on her deathbed. He remembered her as a young woman, as a person to be desired and possessed. Memory provides us this gift, as we grow old. This is what we dream, when memory is free to find its own way without the disturbance of contemporary vision. That same memory inexorably led my father to the vision of some other man in the bed that was rightfully his. Her death did not change this image of his own absence. If time had not eased the memory—it was, after all, more than thirty years back—why should death? If there is an afterlife, my father will be holding on to this unbearable memory forever.

The point of torture is to force the victim to betray comrades and loved ones. My father had wanted my mother to betray herself. She refused. She had forced him to live with her confession and then she simply disappeared. There was no victory to celebrate. Indeed, if there was any victory, it was hers. She had confessed and did not retract, despite his unrelenting attacks. He had survived, but there was no honor in that. There was not even an answer to the question of what to do now. It was again as it had been with the war. He lived; others died. There was no rhyme or reason to the universe. To survive was the only principle upon which he could rely. And how much longer could he even rely upon that?

I wondered if he could go forward without being pulled back to a still-deeper memory. We expect some sort of taking stock after the death of a spouse. Should not the memory of their sixty years together roll over him, bringing comfort alongside the grief? That was what I was feeling: loss in the present, but some comfort from the memory of an entire life. It must have been this feeling that led the ancients to speak of the presence of the spirit of the dead. I did not think my mother was still hanging around suburban Connecticut, but surely, I felt her presence more intensely than I had in the final weeks of her life as she had slipped away. It did not ease the pain. It *was* the pain. Still, it felt right: the presence of absence as the postmodernists might say. We give ourselves over to the memory in order to feel the pain. This is the sacrificial rite we still perform for the dead. We hope for catharsis. We demand of ourselves a period of mourning, because we need this pain to clear a space for the future.

My father, who had always insisted that he had no need of others, now put himself forward not so much as the suffering mourner, but as the suffering old. Without her, he felt old. She had been his life and now that was over. Something of himself had died, leaving him feeling not defeated but deserted. Old age is as much about this stripping away, this being left alone, as it is about physical decline. I was surprised at how quickly he took up this position. He was, from this point forward, needy. No longer making the world tremble with his rage, he started speaking the language of "I can't." "I can't plan the memorial." "I can't respond to neighbors and friends." "I can't decide what to do with the ashes." This from a man who had always filled a room with his presence, who would give orders and make demands. Without my mother, however, there was no one listening to his orders. Apart from his declarations, he did not really know another form of conversation. Whenever he tried small talk, it rapidly left him fuming about how the person he was conversing with was an idiot. He fell silent. He started listening to classical music to fill his time.

The rest of us had to ask whether we would accept the new limits that he was placing around himself. His silence closed off our discourse as well. We failed a moral test when we accepted his terms. In our silence, we broke our bonds to my mother. No one cried at him "shame"; there was no *j'accuse*. We behaved as if we were a normal family and he were simply the aging patriarch. We acted as if he were the central player of a family in mourning. The consolation, if there was any, was that my mother would have wanted it this way. She would not have wanted us to abandon him. Her struggle was about affirming herself in his presence; it was never about destroying him. She always loved him. She had misunderstood the relationship of truth to care. She had been forced to defend herself against his fierce assault. But there was no hatred in her heart. Not for him or for anyone else.

What would have been the point of making the accusation? In fiction, he would have broken down, seeing that his actions had long ago crossed a line from anger to evil. He would have asked forgiveness from those who had loved my mother. Before there could be forgiveness, he would have to perform some sort of penance. He would have made his personal amends to her through whatever ritual could still speak to him. He would have dedicated himself to her memory. Perhaps he would have imposed upon himself a regime of good works. There were those volunteers at the hospice whom he could have joined. Closer to home, he might have invested his concern in his grandchildren. None of this was to be.

His life did approach fiction, but there was no art to it. Art has dramatic unity: it requires a beginning, a middle, and an end. The narrative must be complete for the work to be successful. For my father, there was no such unity. His life was hardly a voyage of self-discovery that would take him back to the truth of love. Her death did not enable him to see a larger meaning. He had no uplifting lessons to share with the rest of us. There was no redemptive moment sought or found.

His life was strictly that of Conrad's Kurtz, even though it played out on the edge of Long Island Sound rather than in deepest Africa. He saw the horror in which all things end. Injustice not civilization; betrayal not love. The fictional quality of his life was limited to the first scene of *King Lear*: rage at what seemed a confession of betrayal. Cordelia said "nothing" to her father; my mother told my father, "You have not been my all." Short of madness, there was no getting over it; neither Lear nor my father could turn back. For my father, there was the insane rage, but there was no epiphany on the fields of Dover as there was for Lear. There was no recovery of the grace of love in the face of death. Life, he thought, was not a moral lesson in the triumph of the good. The sum total of his moral insight was that there are fuckers and fuckees. His life, he thought, had been at the receiving end.

If he did not find his way to redemption, did he at least lie awake wondering what he had done? Did he wish to be able to do it all over? Did he experience some remorse for those final years when he failed to forgive, while he still had the chance? Not ever. Nothing was his fault. Justice was his demand.

This hardly means that he did not feel the shock of her death. Grief neither requires nor brings remorse. His loss was just as real as that of the rest of us. He had been bound up with my mother for all of his adult life. That it came to this was just the way the world was: unjust and without meaning. His life ended where it had begun: with an unjust death. First, it had been his father, now my mother. With his father, he had not yet begun; with my mother, he had not yet been done. In between beginning and end, there was only the threat of death and more injustice. Nothing would change those facts. Yet, it was still his world that had fallen apart with her death.

He was left with an emptiness that opened up a clear view to his own death. No distractions any longer. No one to complain to and no one to complain about. Well, not quite. There were still all the idiots who continually got in his way as he carried out his daily routines. The list of idiots was endless: the kid who packed his groceries, the mechanic who worked on his car, the nurse at the doctor's office, the manager of the condominium complex, and then the politicians who ran the government. No one really cared to listen to this anymore. I learned the art of closing off a conversation without acknowledging what he had said. I did not want to argue with him, but I did not want to support his views. My mother had been both his victim and his audience.

My father knew beginnings, but not ends. He always seemed to be stuck in the middle. He went to war, but never left it behind him. He fell in love and married, but there was no settling into the reciprocity of care. He had a family, but never accepted the generational shift of attention. There could never be any closure in his life because the very idea of closure is a metaphor for death. He was not about to accept the fact of his own death. The past was always a source of injustice, and the future was always the scene of death. He had become a man with neither a useful past nor a hopeful future. He was waiting in the present, but had no belief that a saving power would arrive.

Had my siblings and I assumed our moral debt to my mother and accused him of murderous intent, there is no mystery about how he would have responded. He had never been defeated. He would quickly have recovered his fury and told us again what we had heard for years. That she had sinned against him, that he was the victim. We were idiots if we could not see this. The old battle would be renewed. In the end, he would simply have fled the confrontation. He would have cut us out of his life. But then what life did he have without us? I did not want to imagine him among the homeless. I was not going to change his view of the universe, so I left him alone. There was to be no heart-to-heart talk about the meaning of his loss or the depth of his love. He was again hiding in plain sight.

Those who gathered by the stream were bound to my mother by blood, but so too were we bound to my father. Each of us, at that moment, faced the same inner struggle that had defined my parents' relationship over the last few years: love or justice? We chose love. We would make no trouble for my father. We would grieve the loss of my mother and, for the moment, care for him. I do not think that my mother had been braver than those of us who remained. Not an act of bravery, but of romantic confusion, had set her on the path to confession. Yet, once she found herself in the struggle with my father, she did not give in. She carried on the battle. We failed to take up arms on her behalf. It is easy to betray the dead for the sake of the living.

Our makeshift ceremony by the stream did betray her. Less because we let him get away with murder, than because we failed really to celebrate her world. Talk had animated her world. She had spent a lifetime talking to anyone and everyone. This scene by the river was heavy with what could not be said. For her, blood was only another invitation to talk. Relatives were both figures and players in her endless pursuit of Jewish geography. It was more than a little sad to see that those who gathered were not there because of the bond of talk. Indeed, we were exactly the people who had the least patience with her habit of endless conversation. We, most of all, thought of it as chatter. Quiet by the river was not what she deserved, but a raucous stream of talk in search of points of connection. We were playing the wrong music: somber notes of grief, when she was all about the joyous discovery of the accidental connection.

Not surprisingly, we found that, without her, we did not know what to say. For years, we had left the talk to her. It was, after all, hard to get a word in edgewise when she had the floor. She would pause eventually to let us speak, but then carry on her stream of talk, reacting to what we had said as a pinball might react to a bumper. Had she been there, she would certainly have been the first to speak whatever was on her mind. She would have made the rounds, connecting each of us to all the others. She would have noticed something that reminded her of some connection— perhaps with the site, a stray word, the occasion itself, or most likely just the people there. One thing would have led to another. The silence would have been filled with countless connections. No one was ever alone; all were bound together, if only we stopped long enough to inquire about the comings and goings of families and friends. Had she been there, this ceremony would not have seemed so singular an event. Instead, it would have been caught in a web of meanings that moved backward in time and outward in space. Is not that exactly the point of a memorial?

Years ago, Catherine and I took my mother to a Quaker meeting that was being held as a memorial for Catherine's stepgrandmother, Marjorie. My mother had met her only once or twice over the previous twenty years. She wanted to come along, perhaps more for Catherine's sake than for Marjorie herself. She had never before been to a Quaker meeting. She was among people who had spent their lives with Marjorie, while she barely knew her. I went to support Catherine and to observe this unfamiliar ritual; my mother went to participate. Early on, when a silence descended on the meetinghouse, it was just too much for her. Up she stood and set out her memories of Marjorie. "She was a wonderful woman. She did so much for Catherine." Then she went on to what she had done for her own family, meaning me. She moved on to deeper connections: there was their common experience of the Depression and the War; they were linked in their concern for those who had suffered during the hard period of repressive politics in the 1950s and then through the Civil Rights Movement. Somewhere in this account, there was a further intersection of lives touched: my mother had a friend or a relative who knew the good works Marjorie had done in Philadelphia. On it went. Listening, one would never suspect that my mother barely knew her.

Before she stood up, she had not thought at all of what she would say. She had not jotted down some notes in preparation. She was constructing her memory of Marjorie as she spoke. The real was not the test of her talk; she was making a world for herself and for others. Still, she was not far off—everyone recognized that world as one that Marjorie might have shared. What she had to say was never as memorable as the fact that she was saying it. She had no hesitation, in the midst of a religious ceremony of which she knew nothing, to fill the silent room with her voice. That was her way, and that was what we should have been celebrating—and mourning—on that spring day by the stream. We just did not know how.

We might have benefited from the reassurance of a tradition and the guidance of a professional in such rites of passage. We discover in these moments the usefulness, if not the point, of organized religion. Unwilling to turn to our Jewish traditions, we had no resources upon which to draw. No one among us had any interest in that contemporary form of spirituality: new age faith. No one brought candles or incense. There were no readings from contemporary mystics or those who offer spiritual self-help. Whatever my father might have thought about the religion of his fathers, which was not much, his reaction to new age practices would have been vicious mockery. He would not have been alone in that reaction.

The site by the stream was neither temple nor cemetery. It was nature. I remembered my mother's answer to me years before, when I questioned her faith and she told me, "I believe in nature." Things come around, I thought. Whatever she meant by that, none of the rest of us believed in nature. I like the woods for my customary afternoon walk, but I do not feel particularly close to life there. I like the exercise, not the spirituality. For that, I prefer my books and my own writing.

Despite her answer to my question of faith, not one of us believed that this site by the stream was the right place—the fitting spot—to celebrate my mother's life. Catherine had thought Central Park would have been the better choice, for my mother always thought of herself as a New Yorker. She had certainly been an urban person, unlikely to find herself walking along this stream. New York, however, fell into my father's growing list of "I can'ts." "It is too far. I can't go there." I thought perhaps a memorial garden on some of our land. I imagined a bench with a memorial plaque: a place to sit and think of her life. I did not, however, really expect to find anybody sitting there, and she was not much of a gardener. My sister preferred a boat on the waters of Long Island Sound, but I thought boating was something my father liked and my mother disliked. This was the morbid geography of emotional space. For a person who lived by the word, there really was no right place. We settled on the stream, for it was pretty, close by, and natural.

Disposal of the dead, with all its various meanings, is a task that has only recently been thrust upon us as individuals. Such issues were not previously open to discussion. The dead had their place, even if one believed that their spirits might be everywhere. Now things have turned around: the spirits are gone, and the ashes of the dead can be disposed of anywhere. The park by the house won by default. Having settled on a place, we still had the problem of how actually to do it.

We had brought with us no expert in the performance of ritual. Nor did we check the web for a guidebook or instructions on ad hoc funerals, although it would not surprise me to find that such materials exist. Without any tradition or instruction from which to begin, we put together a shadow of the ritual that once guided the living in taking their leave of the dead. As a shadow, it lacked the main event: the religious assurance that all would be well.

Not until very recently did people gather around the remains of the dead and ask, "What do we do now?" That would literally have been inconceivable. If barely imaginable, it would have registered as a profound moment of social crisis—perhaps of war or disease. Can we really take responsibility for every act in our lives? Must we? There has been set loose upon us an ideal of authenticity: we must make each moment truly our own. The problem is that things do not work this way. At least, not for me.

Not so long ago, lives were measured by rituals that guided us from one phase to another. Today, many of the rituals linger, but no one takes too seriously the idea that they are functioning as rites of passage. They are celebrations without faith. Who believes that the young teenager is about to become a man or that the marriage will last a lifetime? Those who perform these rituals have to swallow hard and hold on to hope that the ritual might provide some contact with a meaningful tradition. For the most part, what had been ritual is today merely celebratory. I am not against celebration, but our celebrations have a smaller compass than in the past. When I attend the bar mitzvah of a friend's child, I am not affirming my faith in the tradition of Abraham. At best, I am affirming my friendship. Attaching the celebratory to the ritual always has, for me, a feeling of inauthenticity. The ritual itself makes no claim, for fundamentally it is not mine.

Recently, I heard of a rabbi who had completely lost his faith. He did not seem to think that faith was a necessary condition of performing the traditional rituals for his congregation. He stayed on. Even for the rabbi, ritual had split apart from faith. So much more so for the rest of us. Faith has become an entirely private matter—more private than religious practice. When I attend these modern versions of traditional rituals, I always wonder who believes the words that are spoken, who even understands the patterns of behavior. When the words become Hebrew, my mind begins to wonder. I lose track of the proceedings and find myself focused on my own speculations—usually theological. This is, no doubt, the philosopher's habit for abstraction. I wonder what everyone else is thinking. I doubt they are thinking of God or even of the history of God's chosen people.

I had just recently seen a working out of the problem of ritual in an age of disbelief at my brother's wedding. On its own terms, it was a success. Certainly, it was a success for my mother. It was her last public outing; her last family celebration. A minister whom they had engaged just for this ceremony performed the ritual. They were not members of her congregation. Before this, I had simply assumed that my brother thought of himself as Jewish. Perhaps he still does. It would not be polite to ask. The minister has become a wedding planner, rather than a spiritual figure. The ceremony itself was rescripted to match their circumstances. It was warm and welcoming, but it followed no tradition. How could it, when the members of my brother's family have all been raised with a visceral reaction against any invocation of "Christ our Lord." I doubt my brother was thinking of conversion, not because Judaism meant something to him, but because no religion meant anything to him.

They wanted the space of the church and they wanted the minister to officiate. They surely did not want the rituals as expressions of a religious tradition, for they lacked the faith that makes sense of those rituals. They embraced the idea that for the ceremony to be authentically their own they must invent the ritual. Wisely, they emphasized the joining of families, rather than the joining of the bride and groom. They adopted a ritual performance that Catherine told me is becoming popular in these circumstances of remarriage. All of their children from their previous marriages were given roles. They came together on the stage holding candles, which they then used to light a single flame. Those present got the idea of "from many to one." I wondered whether it was even right to call this a ritual, since it had been stripped of faith and had no ground in a tradition. But why not? Its function was entirely symbolic and its purpose was to celebrate the transition to a new phase of life.

Not so long ago, a ritual was not read off the internet and accomplished with the purchase of a box of candles. Ritual was anchored in the faith of our fathers. For my brother and myself, our father had no faith. He had no blessing to extend, and his effort to convey a moral lesson failed completely. My brother's wedding had no capacity to promise a future, for there was no community extending its blessing to this marriage. There was literally no community. Those in the church were not a congregation. They were strangers to each other, linked only through their knowledge of my brother, his wife, or their children. The ritual was a performance for the gathering, not an expression of what the gathering could do for them. This is how we live with the remnants of ritual. We still press the pieces into service as if to perform the old miracles. We do not believe, however, that there are any miracles to be had. I, along with everyone else, wished my brother and his new wife well, but that wish was literally all that we had to give them.

An effective ritual, whether of a traditional form or newly invented, has to be more than a cliché, but can it be more than that in the absence of an informing faith? I really do not know. If their marriage is successful, my brother and sister-in-law will look back at pictures of their wedding as the moment that they expressed their love publicly. If the marriage fails, the moment will simply be forgotten. It has no presence outside of their relationship, for it was never about the church, the minister, or the community. It was not a blessing from outside, but the construction of their own blessing upon themselves. What more can we do? Several months later, we found we could do nothing more at our little service by the stream.

There was nothing new for me in this problem of creating ad hoc rituals. My family had passed into the postritual period of modernity before most others. My father had left organized religion for good, after the rabbi failed the bar mitzvah test. He thought of that as a heroic act of enlightenment triumphing over the backwardness of faith. It was also my father claiming authority over his mother, and showing exactly what it meant to grow up without a father.

My mother did not have the strength to resist his evangelical atheism. She was no better than the rabbi had been at answering his questions. They were not married in a temple. My mother loved to remind us that they had been married in what had once been the home of Eleanor Roosevelt in upper Manhattan. Eleanor Roosevelt was a saint in my mother's pantheon.

So it was as I grew up: no temple, no ritual, and no tolerance for those who indulged in the practices of faith. All were idiots. Ritual celebration meant nothing but weakness or maybe the occasion for a party. Despite my father, by the time I finished high school, I was deeply attracted to the idea of faith. I have found in myself a certain religious sensibility. Years ago, I heard a line of poetry while crossing the North Sea: "I am convinced concerning what abides." This captured my enduring sense of a meaningful universe. It is never far from my mind.

Faith hardly eliminates doubt. I share my father's list of questions for the rabbi. I suspect my list is considerably longer than his was. I could not answer them to his satisfaction, but faith abides. It lies in the struggle with doubt. What I have taken over directly from my father is a rejection of all forms of organized religion. He rejected them for their lack of reason. I reject them because they are incommensurate with my faith. Having been brought up outside all of them, none of them "speaks to my condition"—as Catherine's Quaker grandfather would have put it. Mine is a lonely faith for I have neither ritual nor congregation.

Nothing makes me more uncomfortable than an institutionalized ritual. These events are, for me, the least religious moments of my experience. I feel a gap between sacred presence and ritual action. I feel embarrassed even to suggest that, by my actions, I can call forth the sacred. It is not as easy as repeating certain words or motions. For me, such practices appear to be little more than ways of avoiding the genuine struggle of faith. I do not mean to suggest that such words and acts are empty for others. Nevertheless, they are not like a new suit of clothes that one can try on and adopt. Whatever it is that abides in the universe has not granted us such easy access. It takes a lifetime of practice to achieve an enduring faith.

Those without any faith can easily embrace the idea of invented ritual. In their view, there never was any informing god in the traditional ritual practices, so why not adopt them to meet contemporary needs? There is no violation of the sacred in the eclectic borrowing from traditions, for there is nothing that is actually sacred. The past has no privilege over the present. We, no less than our predecessors, want to celebrate the milestones in our lives with friends and relatives. That is all that is at issue; that is all that has ever been at issue. The only appropriate measure of success is the quality of the celebration.

Standing within faith but apart from tradition, I do not feel free to invent my own ritual practices. A religious sensibility can be private. A poem, a story, or even an essay can try to invoke that sensibility for others. A philosophical work can try to understand the nature of the experience. I have written volumes trying to understand the nature of faith. However, one cannot simply make up the acts through which a community—even just a gathering of friends—will experience something of the sacred. Ritual is beyond my ability because it is beyond my capacities. Traditional rituals have been emptied, although I have to confess to feeling a secret excitement when, at the Catholic mass for the dead, I hear the chanting of "he who believes in me shall never die." Invented rituals simply have no place in my experience of the sacred. Both traditional and invented rituals are the sites at which I am most likely to experience the loss of faith. They are, for me, inauthentic.

This gap between faith and ritual paralyzed Catherine and me for many years. We were, I like to say, the last couple of the sixties, having met in 1969. By the early 1980s, we had lived together for many years, but we were not married. That had not been our deliberate plan. We were not "keeping our options open." We simply could not figure out a way to get married in which the ritual would be commensurate with our love. I did not want to experience my own wedding as an inauthentic practice. Looking back, I suspect that this was more my problem than hers. I think she might have happily settled for a white dress, a large gathering of friends, and a memorable meal. To me, none of that sounded right. I wanted the sacrament of marriage; I wanted to receive grace. Unfortunately, I had none of the beliefs that would make that possible in practice.

We fantasized various marriage rituals that might match our sense of love triumphant. We wanted the equivalent of a sacred space. That meant the marriage would have to take place somewhere that held great significance in our lives. Those places were effectively inaccessible to virtually everyone else who would want to be there—especially my mother. My favorite was the top of Mount Hoffman in Yosemite, to be reached only after a long, arduous climb. Catherine preferred southern France. In the end, we just gave up, settling for a bureaucratic procedure in place of a celebratory ritual. We got married by ourselves in a government office that felt to me more like an abortion clinic than a wedding chapel. It had that feel, because it was full of very young couples, some clutching babies, waiting furtively for their turn to go upstairs and stand before the justice of the peace.

Abandoning ritual was no more satisfying than pursuing a failed ritual or inventing an ad hoc ritual. Without faith, however, these are our options: to give up, to invent, or inauthentically to embrace. Catherine and I gave up. My brother invented. Most people I know choose inauthentically to embrace. When my mother died, no one in my family was about to call the rabbi, that left only giving up or inventing.

Giving up was certainly a possibility. It is more common than one imagines once a family decides for cremation. As long as there is an actual body to be disposed of, something must be done. There is a structure to the procedure of burial. No one can get in the gates of the cemetery without making the necessary arrangements. Ashes are another matter entirely. They are given over to the family in a business-like manner. The rest is up to you.

I had gone with my father to get my mother's ashes. The transaction occurred in an office indistinguishable from all the other small businesses on the street. There were a few forms to sign, including an itemized bill—disposal of the pacemaker cost extra. I went because I thought my father should not have to deal with the bleakness of this transaction alone. More importantly, I wanted to make sure that I claimed possession of the ashes as we left the office. I did not want them returning to my father's house. I was not surprised to see how easily he gave them up to me.

But what to do with them? They do not come with instructions, beyond an official certificate that they can be legally disposed of anywhere in the state. They are certified to be environmentally safe. This is no small thing. My father had a deep fear that spreading the ashes might get him arrested. The remains of the dead, despite his absolute rejection of faith, continue to carry a sense of pollution. That ancient idea translated, in his mind, into the modern idea of illegality. That which is not to be touched must be illegal to touch. There is certainly a logic to this: Who could easily accept that spreading around human remains fell within the public health laws? I had tried to reassure him that the law was not a problem, but until he saw the certificate, he refused to believe me.

That the field of possible dispersion has become limitless in no way helps us decide what actually to do. Many people get stuck at just this point. I feared we might. Had the ashes gone to my father's house, we might still be wondering what to do, for the same reasons that it took Catherine and me fifteen years to figure out how to get married. I have heard many stories of people parking the ashes on a shelf and then never getting around to their disposal. It is not that they cannot bear to part with them. Rather, they do not know how to do it. They want a ritual performance commensurate with death, but without faith what might that be? Receiving the ashes in a cardboard box in a transaction at a strip mall certainly helps to drain the aura of the sacred from the event. This business affair is at the far end from the transactions that surround the transfer of the body of the fallen soldier, whose casket is draped with a flag and surrounded by an honor guard. The state still knows the ritual practices that sanctify those who performed the ultimate sacrifice. I wonder how much longer even that memory will last.

Those who receive the cardboard box with the ashes definitely have a disposal problem. The profane character of the whole business overwhelms them. Often, they cannot find their way back to the sacred. They cannot move forward. They discover that the window for the ceremony—any ceremony at all—is actually very short. One cannot call up friends and relatives long after the death to invite them to an ad hoc ritual of disposal. Jews have a rule that a body must be buried within twenty-four hours. There is a lot of sense in that. Grief may last forever, but public displays of grief have a much shorter time horizon. Many people miss the moment. So the ashes sit.

I parked the ashes out of sight on an upper shelf in Catherine's study. I did not want to be reminded of them. I did not want others to know that they were there. I did not want my father to see them when he came to visit. I did not really welcome questions from my kids about Grandma in the box. They had been thinking of that question their entire lives, but always as the hypothetical I posed to them: Would you rather be dead or alive in a box forever? Grandma's ashes in the box were literally a bit too close to home. Instinctively, I was protecting my children from the presence of death, but no more than I was protecting myself.

No less than my father, I felt the ashes to be polluted. Ancient rituals for the dead might no longer be available, but something of the ancient taboos remains. As long as that box was in Catherine's study, crossing the threshold of that room felt like violating a taboo. Leaving the nondescript box of ashes on the shelf in the study was not something I could live with. We would have to invent a ritual.

My only previous experience with an ad hoc ceremony of dispersion had taught me something of the possibilities and the difficulties of invention. Sally's friends had gathered for this final task. It was just the opposite of the scene with my mother: all friends, no relatives. The friends had come from all over the country. Over the time of her illness, they had constituted themselves a real community of care—care for each other as well as for Sally. The very existence of this community spoke to the possibilities of life even in the face of death.

Sally had come into adulthood a very religious person. Her first positions, after college, had been with the social-activist, community-organizing side of progressive churches. Some of her friends came from that tradition. The church, however, was not evident in the ceremony of dispersal planned for the ashes. Too many of her friends had crossed firmly over to the side of the secular. They would have felt excluded by any direct religious reference or traditional ritual.

The ceremony was at a small pond in a wood near her house—a place she liked to walk with her dog. People like to dispose of ashes in water. Effectively, this is just the opposite of the traditional burial in which the body has its own marked space forever. To have such an identifiable location was important as long as the site served as a place of worship. People would go there to revere the ancestors. Think of the tomb of Abraham and Sarah, and the continuing battles in Hebron over what may or may not be that space. No doubt, if we go back far enough, we will find the belief that the tomb or the grave housed the spirits of the dead. But what is the point now? In our digital age, we surely do not need proximity to the bodily remains in order to remember.

My office windows look out on New Haven's historic Grove Street Cemetery. I occasionally see people on the grounds. Some are like me: locals who enjoy a walk on the well-kept, quiet paths of the cemetery. More are visitors, who come to the cemetery after a tour of the university buildings. It is a place of some historical interest. They like to find the graves of the famous. Rarely do I see anyone who seems to have come for a religious or familial purpose. We no longer practice a form of worship at the gravesite. No one has ever said to me that he was going off for an afternoon to sit by the grave of a parent or grandparent. Within a generation, no one in my family will even remember where my grandparents are buried. Already, I do not know. I do not even know whom to ask.

The modern cemetery was invented to be a park-like setting. It took the place of the church graveyard, which kept the bodies of the dead close to the sacred space of the church. Once we gave up the idea of spirits, there was no reason not to seek natural tranquility in place of the protective, but cramped space of the churchyard. The cemetery was to be a space of serenity that would reconnect man to nature. It was, however, a sort of halfway point on the return to nature. Not nature pure, but nature as a product of man's design. The cemetery as park stood in contrast to wilderness. The tranquility and serenity of the cemetery were actually reminders of civilization. Here, death was tamed by culture. Death unbound remained the terror of uncivilized nature. Like every expression of culture, this one too was time-bound. Tastes change, and what seemed so civilized came to appear as just old-fashioned and out of place.

Today, cemeteries are likely to appear as neither tranquil nor natural. With some exceptions, they are more like the strip malls of death. Not high culture, but low. Their aesthetic quality has often been overcome by an absence of urban planning. Most certainly, they do not remind us of the sublimity of nature. They are barely park-like any more. Frequently, development—often suburban—has grown up around them. They bear the same crowded, repetitive appearance as those suburbs. They are neither places of religious sanctity nor places of natural beauty. Worse, there is something vaguely repulsive about the traditional cemetery that shows its master plan in the neat, repetitive rows of graves. The geography of the dead bears too much of the face of administrative rationality. I wonder if I am alone in associating the masses of the dead efficiently buried with the mass graves of twentieth-century genocide. Placing the dead in close proximity to each other seems like a different act after Auschwitz, even when we carefully affix a name to each plot. We want today to free the dead from bureaucratic rationality, regardless of the form it takes.

The military cemetery remains an exception. Here the long rows of graves remind us of the identification of citizen and soldier. On display is not nature, but history. This place is structured by a secular faith in the state: identity and history are written in the landscape. I do not visit the graves of my ancestors, but I do visit those of the war dead. I go to the battlefield cemeteries in Europe and those of our Civil War in order to think about the measure of a life that can give itself up for an idea. In these places, I still capture something of the sacred. I pay my respects to those who found in themselves the strength to sacrifice for a political faith. I remain connected to them by this faith, even though I doubt I have the sort of conviction that could support my own sacrifice. Arlington, however, was not an option for either Sally or my mother. Neither were there any family plots to consider, although I am attracted to that idea: the memorial graveyard of the little platoon that is the family. That idea too, however, is no longer available, for it depended on a practice of patriarchy that settled the matter of which line of descent properly claimed a family: Am I to be buried with my mother's or my father's kin?

The churchyard is gone; the cemetery is passing. The former disappeared when the dead lost their connection with spirits. The cemetery is in trouble at least in part because our paradigm of nature has shifted from the park to the wilderness. That the dead should be returned to nature remains a basic belief for many. The cemetery's capacity to realize that idea has been lost. The cemetery has come to seem quite unnatural; it is a constructed, not a natural, space. We come nearest to communion with the dead, when we allow ourselves to be overwhelmed by the sublimity of nature. Or, so we hope. We no longer fear nature as the threatening wilderness. We have made of it an ideal to counter the frenetic labors of our daily lives. We think it should be peaceful, that it should clear the mind, even if we do not find that effect in ourselves. There was something of this idea in my mother's affirmation of her own belief in nature, years earlier. The need for this belief remained with her, even though I do not think she ever found any peace in nature. She was urban to the core. Noise settled her mind; stillness made her panic.

The strong inclination to distribute ashes in water comes from this sentimental belief in nature. The indefinite character of water suggests a oneness with all that is. It symbolizes the flow of time and thus the inevitable loss of personal identity. No marker or physical presence awaiting the second coming and the call to bodily resurrection. No God, but only nature untamed. The aesthetics of nature is to stand in for the spiritual. Or perhaps it is better to put it the other way around: we find the spiritual wherever we can. Without faith in the traditions of our grandparents, we look to nature.

Nature does not leave us without resources for a sustaining faith. Not long ago, I found myself on the beach with an artist friend. We got there at sunset. Ordinarily, I do not have much of a visual imagination, but on this evening, I was quite overwhelmed by the beauty of the western sky. I turned to her and said that we were witnessing "an aesthetic proof of the existence of God." Evolutionists may be able to defeat the argument from design. They can explain how something as complicated as the eye could evolve from simpler structures, given enough time. The beauty of this sunset, however, was beyond their explanatory power. We could not help but look on in awe. We could not help but believe that this beauty was for us. We could no more imagine it as a random event than we can imagine that proverbial monkey pecking away at a typewriter forever and finally producing *Hamlet*. We had to see this sunset as the product of an aesthetic sensibility.

The sublimity of that sunset has displaced the beauty of the nineteenth-century park as our ideal of nature. It is the untouched, not the man-made, that moves us. Lacking religious faith, we are still drawn to the sublime. That is what we hope to find in nature. That is how we got to the pond in the woods by Sally's house. We had the place but not the ritual. Sally's friends, however, turned out to be good at this. That some were deeply religious no doubt helped. More than that, the fact that they were a community of care came out. I found myself moved by the words and song, even if I felt myself to be more bystander than participant. What they were not able to accomplish, however, was the actual ritual of dispersion. Here, things quickly fell apart. The absence of ritual—a well-tested practice—threatened to turn the whole event into comedy.

No one had actually thought through the physical steps of disposal. The opportunity for the sublime quickly slipped into something all too profane. The ashes had been brought in a plastic bag. The only tool anyone had to spread them was a plastic spoon. It was as if someone had searched the drawer in which picnic supplies were kept to find the tools for disposal of the dead. In some respects, it had become just another trip to the pond. The sublime can quickly slip into the natural, and the natural into the ordinary. This was, after all, just the pond near Sally's house.

It was our poor luck to find a hard wind blowing off the pond when we got there. How exactly does one dispose of ashes in a strong wind? No one had thought about this. We were not professionals; we did not have a contingency plan. We had our plastic spoon and that was it. We had no waders to get out away from the edge of the water. No canoe or rowboat. No point of access to water flowing in or out of the pond. We were all people of the arts, with little practical sense it turned out. We started releasing the ashes, but they were quickly blown on to all of us gathered at the pond's edge. Soon we were all bearing bits of Sally on our clothing. This was not working. It ended quickly with a very unceremonious dunking of the contents of the bag into the water. They were released at a point so close to the edge that they just clung to the shoreline. We did not linger in that spot. I remember the event through this image of little eddies of Sally's ashes, trapped along the shore.

I had learned one lesson from Sally's ceremony: the water must be moving. Thus, the stream with the little bridge. I had also learned enough to buy a nicely made spoon for the occasion. No picnicware. These were problems I could solve. I was far less able to solve the problem of what to do. We needed still to construct a ritual for people who had no tradition to guide them and no faith to unite them. It would have helped to have some shared sense of what this was all about, apart from the pressing fact that something had to be done.

Saying goodbye was not really what was at stake, although I did use just that word at the end. It is actually strikingly appropriate, for the expression is a contraction of "God be with you." I wished I could say that with the same faith from which the expression arose. If any of us had believed in a watching God, then we would have known what to do. Whatever the content of my faith, or that of anyone else by the stream, none of us believed there was any more left of my mother than the ashes we poured into the water. Without remains, she was without remainder. This was certainly not a ritual for the dead in any literal sense. Nor was it about closure, as if we could relieve grief by coming together. No memorial service is about the end of mourning. It is rather a part of the mourning. We want the support of others who have also suffered the loss; we do not yet want relief from the loss. Remembering together is a way of being with others while continuing to feel the loneliness of loss. Death can bind us to others, even as it leaves us reeling in loneliness.

Our made-up ritual by the stream, however, was not enough to create the bonds of a community of care among those who fundamentally did not care for each other. Despite the fact that we were related, we were splintered. Sally's friends were more of a community than our small group of relatives. We had not drawn together during my mother's illness, and now even that motivation was past. We struggled to find the words that seemed right. No words seem right when they are asked to bear the weight of a death without a supporting faith.

The right words are those that none of us knew how to say: the words of ritual that carry with them the magic of faith. These words remind us of how countless generations have come to this same point, of how they came together over a death, and of how they extended to the dead what was owed. They tell us that there is nothing new in this situation, that the world goes on and so will we. They remind us of who we are and that we are together.

By that stream, we had no sense that we were part of a tradition. We were there precisely because we lacked a tradition. Without a past, we had no future together. This spot would not bear the memory of my mother's death. Our very act of memorializing was constructed in such a way as to guarantee that it would not be remembered. It left no physical mark, no trace at all. In truth, it would not even be remembered by the participants for long. We did not know how to make something out of nothing, which is just what the ritual for the dead must do.

Without traditional texts to guide us, we looked for their secular equivalents in poetry or song. We could not create the sacred, but could we even create theater? Theater shares with the sacred the character of suspending disbelief. For the space of a performance, we forget the staged character of what we see. We become participants in the world set before us, accepting its meanings and its possibilities. We care about these characters, wanting them to succeed in that world we share with them for the duration of the play. We look back at a successful performance exactly for this sense of the extraordinary. There, we saw something not available in ordinary life. We caught a glimpse of a different world, a different set of meanings, which remind us that we are not limited to our everyday concerns. Part of our nature is to overflow the chores of daily life, to see through that life to larger patterns of meaning. We are never exhausted, or used up, by what we have been and what we are doing. Our possibilities always exceed our accomplishments. That surplus was once captured in the idea of a soul that was never exhausted in this world.

Even by the measure of the theatrical, we did not perform all that well. Did we reach that point of suspension of disbelief; did we catch a glimmer of the infinite? Did we find in that natural setting an expression of the aesthetic proof of the existence of God? No. We came together, knowing we would quickly be on our way. There was not even a sense that this was a final gathering, marking the end of the long story that was my mother's life. Several participants read poems. My aunt read some pages of a little essay that my mother had written some years back on her own coming to America. I read a few pages from a book of mine. They were pages I had written thinking about the death of one of my closest friends a few years back. They tried to describe the presence of love at the deathbed scene. All of this failed to overcome the sense of inauthenticity of role. We were doing this, but we were not really this. We could not remind each other of deeper bonds when they were not there.

Most striking was the absence of shared memories of my mother. Catherine was, as usual, the bravest of us all, speaking of how my mother would light up at the sight of us even when she could no longer speak. The rest of us did not go in this direction because there was one memory—*the memory*—that could not be spoken at all. The memory of the struggle with my father, of what had set it off, and of how it had reached no conclusion. We had silently agreed not to speak the truth that could not help but be on our minds.

We all came to this event not so much intending to speak of our memories, but wanting to know what exactly my father would say. We were looking to him for an account or perhaps an accounting. We were not prepared to accuse him, but we all turned our gaze upon him. There was not much chance that he would speak simply as the mourning husband. There was no chance that he would speak directly to the group, expressing his love for us or thanking us for our support. There was, of course, the real possibility that he would simply flee, that he would effectively say nothing but just turn away from the eyes focused on him. That is what I expected, but not what happened.

He chose two poems to have read. He did not think that he was up to the reading, so he asked my uncle. Remarkably, the two poems were in German. Perhaps my aunt and uncle understood, but no one else. No explanation from my father. No translation was offered. I wondered how these poems might have figured in his earliest years with my mother. Did he have something of the romantic in him after all? How could he not? After all, the whole of his struggle with my mother had come out of his feeling of an unbearable betrayal. He must have been remembering the very deep past. A world so distant that the rest of us were barred by language itself from entering. More than that, we were not invited. By choosing German, he was excluding us from this part of his relationship with my mother. The memory of his love was not something to be shared. It was not to be celebrated with others. It was revealed but remained secret even in its revelation. He could not even speak it himself.

I suspect that he had planned nothing further than my uncle's reading of the two German poems. He had solved the puzzle of how simultaneously to flee and to participate. He would be there and not there. He would hide in plain sight. The strategies of a lifetime become second nature. Something, however, pulled him further into the ceremony. He found himself unable to stay quiet. If the poems were a puzzle, what he said next was shocking. He spoke no further of love. Instead, he said that he always felt as if his relationship to my mother was one in which he was doing "penance" for what the Nazis had done to her family.

We were back at the scene of my brother's wedding. He could not think of love, without thinking of justice. The poems were the memory of love. The secret to a long marriage, he had said, was love. This memory of love had never disappeared. It was for him, however, a source not of happiness, but of pain. It may have been the foundation, but it was never enough. It could never rise up to build the structure of a life together. It did not protect them from an unjust world. Love for him could be glimpsed, but it could not be spoken. As soon as he started to speak, he would turn from love to justice. Is this not the story of his rage over all those years? Whatever the meaning of love, it was entirely private. In the public world, the world that appeared as soon as he spoke, love was always displaced by justice.

In the park, we saw again that his sense of justice was metaphysical. For him, things did not just happen. There was no merely accidental quality to life, no random pattern of events. Justice and injustice—mostly injustice—were the very frame of history, the secret pattern of the way of the universe. His life, he now said, had been a call to do justice. His war had never ended. It was unjust that he had been forced to bear the burden of the Nazis' actions when he was called to risk his life at war. Somehow, he thought that he continued to bear that burden in his relationship to my mother.

What an odd confusion of roles, I thought. Here he was, a Jew born in America who had fought the Nazis to liberate Europe. Yet, what did he think made the deepest claim upon his sense of justice? To do penance for the destruction that the Nazis had done to the German Jews. It would be easy to think that his sense of responsibility for the Germans arose out of a prewar fascination he had had with all things German. He had, after all, been at the very head of his high-school class in German. Had he personally been let down by the nation of Goethe and Hölderlin, by the culture that had produced Gödel and Einstein? There may have been some of this lost innocence years before, but it was no longer at the heart of the matter.

Nor was it that he felt himself to be part of the vast military effort that had destroyed Germany and then assumed the obligations of government immediately after the War. Something was indeed owed to the Jews by Germany, and for a short while that obligation was transferred to the victors who became responsible for Germany. My father had spent much of his life denying his Jewishness. I do not think he could easily identify with the Jewish victims of the war. But that hardly left him on the other side, thinking he had inherited the obligations of the vanquished. Nor was it simply that the civilization of the enlightenment had done this to the Jews and my father thought himself as the embodiment of reason. I am sure he did not think of the Nazis as enlightened. They sought to destroy the culture of reason that he so valued.

My father often gave the appearance of caring for no one. He could explode against those he loved. He was, at best, indifferent to those with whom he came in contact in his daily life. He thought the world inhabited by two kinds of people: those who were deliberately unjust and those who were too dumb to know that they were being victimized. Often, he did not know with which group he was angrier: the rich who took advantage or the poor who failed to defend themselves. He ended up angry with both. He did not believe anybody who suggested that the powerful could be reformed or the victims could be educated. Always, there would be the fuckers and the fuckees.

Where was my mother in this scheme? Until she betrayed him, she was innocent. That is always the meaning of love. When my father made fun of my mother's lack of a sense of space and of her practical confusions, he was affirming her innocence. The innocent do not belong in this world. The object of our love is always innocent because love does not speak to the world of justice and injustice. Love creates its own world of meaning, which has nothing to with the structure of justice. Falling in love with my mother, my father saw innocence in an otherwise terrible world. That the world could do what it had done to her was unfathomable and unacceptable. We all want to protect the object of our love from the world. Do we not all feel deep down that we are of the world while the person we love is innocent? Do we not all feel that we must do penance for what the world—our world—does to those we love? He would bear the weight of this world to protect her. His deepest feeling was that he had to make up for the injustice of the world. This was the source of his sense that he was performing penance.

The burden for which he thought he had to do penance was the burden of the entire twentieth century. No matter how much the ancient Jews suffered at the hands of history, they thought that they must do penance for their failure to succeed. In their world, only God controlled the movement of history. If they suffered, it must be because they were not innocent. My father had reached a similar conclusion about his own life of suffering. It could not be that this was simply the working of chance. His universe, like that of his forefathers, was moral all the way down. Injustice had to be explained. It had to be turned into an offering. "Take me, not the innocent," the ancient martyr said to his God. So my father spoke to an unjust universe in which there was no longer a God listening to his prayer. All of his suffering, he now suggested, was a suffering for others. My father, who always appeared to us as a vengeful God and to himself as a victim, was telling us now that he had been the martyr.

From a man who had spent the last five years of his life in a murderous rage at my mother, this was hardly convincing. He had been doing penance? I thought he still had substantial penance to perform—at least in the moral universe I inhabit. Of course, he was not thinking of the last five years. He was thinking back to the beginning. He was remembering the long years of marriage when he did not flee, although he desperately wanted to. He was thinking of the commitment he had made and what it had felt like then. To me, it always seemed that my father could not commit himself to anything. He always seemed in restless flight. To him, it seemed he was always restraining his desire to flee. Each time he stepped back over the threshold of home, he thought this was the penance he must pay, the burden he must assume, for the violation of innocence that had been done to the object of his love. "I give myself," he thought.

In this immoral world, he had taken a stand. This was the myth he had constructed out of his love. He had rescued her; he had suffered for her. In the face of world-historical injustice, he had done his part. He would not contribute to the evil of the world. He would give himself up for the sake of innocence. He was morally bound not to add to the suffering of the Jews. In this case, "the Jews" meant my mother. His life had been a rescue mission. That the rescuer can become the victimizer should not be surprising. The step from penance to revenge was instantaneous at the moment he heard my mother's confession.

To do penance is ordinarily to give something up in order to overcome a moral debt. My father did not think he had sinned, but he did think there was a moral debt to be paid. If my mother had found her way to confession, had this evangelical atheist somehow found his way to Christ? Was not Christ's sacrifice a penance paid for the sins of others? I had to remind myself, once again, that the religions of the West are bred deeply in the bone. Is that not the story of my family, including myself?

In my father's mind, he had taken on a burden of suffering, because he would not abandon my mother. His suffering must be for her; he bore that cross. He believed this, but my father never understood himself. He was offering a final explanation of why it was that he found himself at age eighty-three, the fuckee: he was doing penance. At this particular moment, at this spot by the stream, with my mother's ashes still in the urn beside me, this mythic explanation from my father was incomprehensible. It has taken me years to understand. In his own odd way, he was asking for our sympathy. His life, as much as hers, he was saying, bore the tragedy of the twentieth century. That part he had right.

At the wedding, he had told us that there is a natural moral order within a marriage: he had tried to be an "enlightened despot." At the memorial, he told us he had been doing penance all these years for the unjust suffering of my mother as a child. With rule comes responsibility.

He had to rule and to protect, even if it meant his own sacrifice. He was the ancient ruler, standing between his nation and their god. He would bring enlightened rule, but he would also offer himself for the sins of the world. Without a god to take the offering, however, his penance was an empty act. It could protect no one. Most of all, it had not protected my mother from him.

Instead of creating a world of care, this thought of his own penance fueled his resentment when he learned that she was herself the source of the greatest injustice in his universe. He had been mocked, his kingship denied, his act of penance ignored. He had sacrificed for nothing. This was the source of his raging, endless fury over my mother's confession. My father became the Robespierre of family life. He thought he was bringing the enlightened rule of reason, but he ended up bringing the terror. Robespierre, too, probably went to the guillotine thinking he was doing penance for a nation that had failed him.

We stood by the stream stripped of the sacred. There was no moral discourse to which we could turn to understand my father's claim for recognition of his life of penance or my sense of his own injustices. We found no relief in nature, and no vision of the sublime. We managed to create no ritual to remind us of our common bonds, for the truth was that we had very few. We needed faith, but felt only its absence. In this silence of failed ritual, we disposed of the ashes. I said "Goodbye, Mom," and my brother repeated the words. The stream took them away quickly. She was gone. We did not linger. There was no sitting shiva, there was only a brief lunch after which everyone went on their way. We were done, not just with this ceremony, but done as a family. It had always been my mother who had bound us together. My brother and sister would help in the care of my father, but there would be no family reunions across the generations. No celebrations of family history and future. The horizon of family memory has shrunk. None of us will endure beyond the memory of our grandchildren.

My father too went back to his home. He lived on. He would go months without mentioning my mother, and then suddenly he would say to me that he was still suffering from the loss or that he thought of her always. He would say he was puzzled as to why other people did not speak about her. I did not believe him. He never brought up the subject of a larger memorial event. He tried flirting with some of the widows around the condominium. It did not work out very well. He would call me and tell me that he really did not like "old women." He had few friends for he really had no idea of how to be with people. My mother had always taken care of that. He would inevitably start belittling whomever he was with. No one understood the real injustice of the world. They were all idiots.

He added to his list of "I can'ts." I would try to ignore it. I thought it good for him to continue to care for himself. He should walk, clean, cook, and shop. As long as he could drive safely, I was not going to yield. I saw no benefit in his giving up or fleeing from life one last time. I was not prepared to be too sympathetic, for while he might not mention her, I could not be with him without thinking of my mother. I never asked for an explanation, and I never accused him. Love or cowardice? A bit of both.

I try to have dinner with him once a week. I have stopped asking Catherine to join us. She does not enjoy being with him or being in the home that reminds her of my mother. Over dinner, I try to move away from his complaints about body and mind. We talk of politics or about the failing economy. I want him to exercise his mind, as well as his legs. I talk to him about the success and failure of my children. He thinks he should be interested, but he is not really. He never talks to me about his other grandchildren. They simply do not cross is mind. He rails against the injustice in the world; that is his exercise. Catherine tells me that she is sure that he is afraid of death, just as he has always been. Death must increasingly fill his vision as friends and relatives fall away. I am sure Catherine is right, even though this is not a subject that ever comes up when I speak with my father. It too is hiding in plain sight.

I drive home from these weekly dinners, wondering what to make of all this pain in the last few years. I know that there could not have been such pain without love. I know that love is the hardest thing in the world, for as I told my friend many years ago, we see our own death in those we love. Love is both resource and threat. For my father, it became all threat. He never got through his sense of betrayal; he never arrived at the far shore to find again the resources of love. He is a man without faith in a universe that offers no care, but only injustice and death. Can we live in that world, I wonder? Can we stare at death and injustice and bear up under the weight? Can we simply pitch in and do our best, as if life is a project at summer camp? My father could not, and I am quite sure I cannot either. My father resisted it with all the passion of a furious will. I resist with a faith in what abides.

Faith is never just a proposition; it is never the conclusion of an argument. This is what my father demanded of his rabbi many years ago. Measured by reason, faith is always absurd. My father was convinced he had won the argument. Anyone who failed to see that truth was either too dumb or too weak. That faith might require strength was not a concept he could grasp. He thought that belief had to be conditioned by understanding, and that whatever could not be understood was simply illusion. We must free ourselves from all such illusions and rely on reason alone. That reason led him to madness, that it was wholly incommensurable with the world in which he found himself, was never apparent to him. He thought he was the measure of reason in an unreasonable world.

Faith is, by definition, unreasonable. We cannot reason ourselves to faith. It is not a set of answers to questions—my father's or anyone else's. Even the catechism is more than a set of propositions. It is repeated in a ritual that frames a life. These actions lead the faithful into the world; they give structure to that world. With structure can come a sense of being at home in a world that is one's own. Faith is never anything more or less than a way of being in the world. We find faith in our actions, not in our arguments. It compels us in the same way the laws of gravity compel us: this is the way the world is. Often we do not know whether we have faith until we look to see what we have done and must do. Abraham had faith when he prepared to sacrifice Isaac. Could he have known in advance that he would do the deed? No. He learned who he was at the moment he lifted the knife. He learned that his world is not reasonable; it is not one that he could understand. The meaning of that world only became clear in his act: faith, he learned, is greater than life itself. This is not a unique lesson. Every time the soldier charges into the battle, he learns that his world is one of faith beyond reason. To remember this, I visit Gettysburg.

Modern moral philosophy misses the character of faith, when it makes a strict separation between the is and the ought. No moral proposition—a statement about what is good or bad—follows from a proposition about what is the case. We cannot learn what should be from what is, any more than I can learn what I want to order for dinner from reading the menu. I cannot learn what I should do with my life from looking at the talents I happen to have. The point is self-evident, except that it misconceives the way in which we experience the world. We do not find ourselves in a world stripped of value. Instead, we find ourselves in a world of care. We are pulled into this world because we care about it. This is not a matter of reason. We must suspend disbelief; we must give up the crutch of reason. We must have the courage to be that which we find in ourselves. We must say with Abraham, "here am I." These words proclaim an openness to the sacred. I will construct nothing; I will demand nothing. Yet, I have faith.

Faith places us in a world in which the is and the ought converge. We live in and with faith—or we do not. It is not true or false, any more than love is true or false. We cannot argue ourselves into love any more than we can argue ourselves to faith. Lovers may not know what to say to each other; they express their love in their touch, their gaze, their mutual silence. Finding ourselves in a world in which the sacred makes a claim upon us, we know how to respond. That response is the beginning of ritual, whether it is formal or not. Without faith, ritual cannot bear its own weight. It will appear instead as an inauthentic expression, like a role in a play that we may take up or leave behind. The role is never me, no matter how suitable it may seem.

I call my faith love. There is no longer a caring God, but our lives are still filled with the sacred. We are born into families and communities; we fall in love and find ourselves in a new world. We are not asked to decide whether the people we love will have a meaning for us. We do not check their values against our own, as if love must be predicated on some agreement. We do not pick the objects of our love. They claim us. We long with all our hearts to fall in love. We want to be claimed completely by a love that makes us blind to calculation, and makes us forget ourselves in the other. Nothing is worse than to find ourselves in a world without love. Not health, not reason, not entertainment can make up for the absence of love. If there is love, then there is still faith. We are convinced by what abides.

The action of love is sacrifice. This is just what the story of Abraham tells us. It is what our national history tells us as well. To love, we must give up ourselves. That giving up is simultaneously a taking on. We give up the finite and take on the infinite. Couples have their own rituals, as do parents and children. These are the actions of love—intimations of sacrifice. They are not means to some other end; they are rather the way in which we live in a meaningful world. Without faith and the rituals it spawns, we would not have the courage to see our own death in our children. When I would read to my daughter beside her bed each night, I would feel that I was giving up myself to her. This was literally a moment of transfer made possible in our nightly ritual. She will live; I will die. This was the text I read behind the words of the children's book. When I would sit into the early morning with my other daughter as she cried in her resistance to sleep, and I would repeat the mantra, "this is a privilege," I was performing another ritual of sacrifice. "My life for yours," I was saying.

In and through those we love, we have already died to ourselves. We have become one through a faith that abides. If you cannot take up this thought of sacrifice, then you will turn on the object of your love. You will resent the demands of love. You will see only demands and not the claim of care. You will measure those demands as unjust. Indeed, they are unjust. Because they are, love is always an exercise in forgiveness.

If we seek to measure the objects of our love by the standards of justice, they will always fail. This is what Jesus meant when he reminded his listeners that they have all sinned. We must come to love ready to forgive and ready to be forgiven. We must create the world anew as one that shows forth a meaning beyond the measure of justice. We want together to catch that glimpse of the infinite, to experience the sublime. If we cannot, we are doomed. That which we must believe, we can believe. To get there, however, requires a courageous act of faith.

I do not know if my father ever loved. I am inclined to think he did. I also think he found he did not have the courage of faith. He was asked to sacrifice in the war. He realized then that he did not believe. No one can condemn him for that. It is tragedy, not moral fault or failure. We cannot compel faith or demand its presence where it does not exist. Gods die and when they do, we come to believe they never existed. That is the nature of faith: it exists, until it does not. The whole point of faith is that we do not know how we will act until such moments are upon us. That is the test of faith.

My father lost whatever capacity for faith he had. Love was never enough for him because he could not suspend disbelief. He thought he was bravely facing the real world, but in truth, he lacked the courage to love. My mother loved. She loved the whole of the human world around her. She loved it in its detailed connections that were always a marvel to be discovered and treasured. She did not understand much of justice; she understood nothing at all of truth. She had faith that love would carry her through. For this belief, she suffered greatly. Between my mother's pain and my father's rage, I would choose love over justice. My father, who deeply rejected Judaism, remained a Jew to the end. His son, who rejected every form of organized religion, had become a Christian.

The people we love make a claim upon us. They show us that there is a meaning to the world, which is beyond our powers of comprehension. Through them, I learn who I am. They enlarge my soul to the point at which I can say, "I am a part of all that I experience." They take me into the world and I know that it is good. It is good even as it is unjust. The injustice I hope to help fix; the goodness I know has little to do with me. I know all of this with a certainty that no reason can shake. I know it so deeply that I mourn our common fate. I know our world is here only for a limited time. It may seem a long time, but it is never enough time for the infinite value that is here. The puzzle in my life is not that injustice can exist in a world that is good, but that this world that is good will come to an end. About this, I have been in mourning as long as I can remember.

This is faith without myth. Can we love in a world that is as doomed as each of us is doomed? Can we find our way to the infinite in a finite world? This is the real struggle of faith with doubt today. I do not know if we can, but I am convinced that we must.

Killingworth, Connecticut, Summer 2009

Coda

Ten years later, we gathered again at the same stream in the park. Our band was smaller, but our task was the same. We were there to distribute my father's ashes. My brother and sister each spoke, making the best they could of my father's difficult life. I said nothing. My anger at my father was now without bounds. I had opposed having any sort of memorial event. When my siblings insisted, I agreed to attend. I wanted to be done with him.

My cousin, who was there in place of his parents who had been at my mother's service, described the event as a "celebration of life." I was not in a celebratory mood. I thought of my mother; I thought of the memorial service my father never had for her. Did I owe him this, to forgive his trespasses? He never forgave anyone their trespasses against him. Where was the lesson in love I had taken from my mother's death?

I was, by the time of his death, well beyond my capacity to forgive. To speak truthfully, I wanted this man erased from memory. In the last two years of his life, he had turned toward me the unrestrained hatred he had directed at my mother. I had done my best to support him as he physically declined, yet I became the object of an endless rage that knew no bounds. He threatened me with physical injury, even as he was losing his strength. He often sat before me in stony silence, turning red in the face and sweating profusely as he suppressed an explosion of fury. Then, the explosion would come. I thought of my mother often and of how terrible her final years must have been. I may be a philosopher, but I am not a saint. I endured, but I could not forgive.

After my mother's death, my father lasted about two years in their condominium. We all urged him to move into a nearby assisted-living facility, but he resisted. He always feared change; he would make do. Once a week, I would visit, usually bringing dinner. We talked politics more than anything else. He had no patience for small talk, but he also resisted abstraction. Small talk included any talk about his children or grandchildren; abstraction included anything on which I was working. Politics fell into the middle range. It allowed him to vent at all the "idiots."

He knew a few people in his complex and they seemed to have gotten over the very public war he had conducted with my mother. Nevertheless, he found himself the awkward third, even with his few friends. Mostly, he was alone. He resisted moving to an assisted-living community because it was unmistakably a final move. One moves there as part of a plan that includes only one form of departure at the far end. That was not yet a plan he was prepared to make.

Eventually, he gave in. I took him to visit two assisted-living communities in the area. One was a bit more upscale. He chose the other for reasons that had nothing to do with lifestyle. The upscale facility had quite a few residents who had been university professors. Some had been my colleagues. My father had no interest in competing with them. Professors had authority; he only had his opinions. He needed to be the smartest person in the room. He would stay away no matter how nice the accommodations were.

I was completely surprised by how easily and quickly he took to the new place, once he made the move. During his first few years in his new apartment, he was happier than I had ever seen him. I felt a burden had been lifted from me. No longer did I feel a need to bring dinner weekly or even to check in by telephone most days. He was busy.

Soon, he had a girlfriend with whom he would eat dinner every night. He started going to concerts, both in the building and out. I would run into him coming out of the concert hall on campus, as he made his way back to the facility's bus. He took charge of a film group. He went to lectures; he held forth at discussions of public events. He seemed to get along with other residents. To my complete shock, he even started to care for some of them, noting if they were not well or recommending various activities. Could my father be a normal person after all? Was it just that he did not get along with my mother? Had they simply been ill-suited for each other?

I tried to understand this change in my father. He never spoke of the past; he never mentioned my mother. He was content with the present. For a man who could never settle down, who was haunted by his past, this was surprising. For a man who desperately feared death, it was even more surprising. Now people around him were regularly dying. He did not mention this. I would lose track of people that I thought he liked in the community and have to discover for myself that they had passed on.

Life in the new community, I concluded, had a familiar and comforting feeling for my father. He was back to his childhood as the exceptional son in a household of women who spoiled him. Assisted living must have felt like his life around the time of junior high school. The time before the War, the family, and the affair.

My father was one of the few men in the assisted-living community. Of those men, extraordinarily few were unattached. He was suddenly the object of attention from many women. They wanted to have dinner and a glass of wine or maybe go to a concert. They wanted to care for him. They would willingly listen to his opinions on everything; they rarely disagreed. They accepted his view of his own exceptional qualities. They wanted to be seen with him. It made them feel normal again. They could see that he was well-read and that he did not spend his time on games, sports, or entertainment. In their view, he was a serious man who needed their help. He was, after all, a recent widower. What could he know about taking care of himself? He basked in this attention.

I compare this experience to his life in junior high school, not high school, for one simple reason. It was female companionship and care without the anxiety that he felt around sex. His infantilization by his mother and older sister had done permanent damage. He had endlessly accused my mother of being a whore. His problems with sexuality, however, ran deeper than the affair. They began with his discomfort with the body itself. It was, after all, the instrument of death. Approaching ninety, he enjoyed all the female attention, but he really did not care much for these new women in his life. He went out of his way to tell me that they threw themselves at him. He told me he had no particular interest in them and no interest whatsoever in sex with them.

I once mentioned something about sex among the elderly to the facility doctor. He told me that I should make no assumptions about their sex lives. I do not, but he did not know my father, who was confiding to me things that I did not want to hear. He would tell me that he did not find older women attractive and he rejected their physical advances. He was making excuses, trying to justify his flight from sexuality. The difference between his ninety-year-old self and his earlier self was that he now found it easier to believe the excuses. He was, he told himself, simply enjoying the dinner conversation and the companionship. He genuinely liked appearing as the man with a date. He was exceptional again, as he had been when he was Capt'n Sam. That his companion might want more from him was not something with which he was concerned. When his first companion became ill, he quickly abandoned her. She faced death without his support. I learned later from the doctor that this had upset her greatly at the end.

Things went well enough until his ninetieth birthday. By then, he was unsteady in his movements and fearful of being away from his building. There were always issues about finding and using public bathrooms. Better not to take the risk. He finally gave up his car. For his birthday, my brother announced that he had reserved a large table at a local restaurant. He had invited the siblings and grandchildren for a celebration. I told Catherine that I did not think this a good idea given my father's limited maneuverability. I also told her that I was sure that, one way or another, my father would not attend.

We received a call from the health center at his facility early in the morning on the day of the dinner. My father could not get out of bed. He had a debilitating attack of vertigo. Soon, he was in the hospital for tests and observation, and Catherine and I were on our way there. He stayed three days as the doctors tried the various procedures regularly used to get the inner ear back in line. They had no success; they could find no cause of his condition. More puzzling to them, his range of symptoms did not match those that ordinarily accompany the condition. I was confident that the entire episode was psychosomatic.

My father's history of trauma stood as a testimony to the power of his psyche to take control of his body. The insomnia, the cold sweats, the physical outbursts all occupied a space in which the physical and the psychological could not be separated. He genuinely suffered from his memories; he suffered in the most physical of ways. I never considered it, but he had a history of rashes and obesity that also spoke to the power of his mind over his body. Before the end, he would partially lose his vision to the same power of psychosis. Like Oedipus, he would blind himself, rather than look at what he had become. For years, he had thought he could will himself to health. In truth, he was more successful at willing himself to illness.

To say, then, that his vertigo was a psychosomatic condition did not make it any less real. He really could not get out of bed without collapsing from dizziness. The psychological origin made the condition more, not less, difficult to treat. In fact, he never really recovered. The elderly, I learned, can lose their strength very quickly. Once gone, it is very difficult to recover.

On his return from the hospital, he went straight to the health center, where he remained for the next month. He continued to have attacks of dizziness. It was as if he had forgotten how to steady himself. He had trouble with his knees and little energy. He stopped eating regularly. He expanded yet again the range of his "I can'ts." To virtually every suggestion from the physical therapist or from me, his response would be "I can't do that." We made him try.

He now thought of himself as old and disabled. I did not believe that he could change so much over the course of a week or two. I urged—actually insisted—that he get up and do things for himself. He resisted. The in-house doctor joined me in my rejection of his self-pity. I quite liked this doctor. When my father first entered his care, he was optimistic in his prognosis. He told me that he had dealt with my father on occasion and he seemed a nice man in relatively good health for his age. I told him that he would soon learn that my father was anything but nice.

While the staff worked very hard to help my father recover, he had nothing but disdain for them. He alienated and infuriated everyone he met in the health center. He was, as I had long observed, incapable of thanking anyone. He thought the nurses and orderlies who took care of him were only doing their jobs, for which they deserved no special recognition. He complained endlessly about the young women who cleaned his room and served him meals. He accused them of not treating him properly and of stealing from him. Very quickly, none of the staff had any interest in being near him. What sort of care could he expect, when he constantly abused those trying to help? I had to intervene frequently.

He trusted just one aide who was a large, kind, middle-aged black man. I suspect my father feared him. Before the end, my father would hallucinate that even this kind man was extorting money from him. He desperately directed me to write him checks, fearing what might happen to him in the shower, if we did not do so. The aide did his best to reassure my father, but he was beyond reassurance.

Several weeks after he was admitted, the doctor told me that while he had occasionally seen patients like my father, all of them had been abandoned by their families. He posed to me the question with which I struggled for the next few years: Why did I continue to care for my father? Was there a moment when I should simply have walked away? What exactly does a son owe his father, when the relationship turns murderous?

The doctor shared my view that the vertigo was as much a psychological as a physical condition. He wanted to treat my father aggressively. He made him get up and walk; he made him exercise. He insisted that he take his meals in the dining room, rather than in bed. My father quickly came to hate him. He accused the doctor of trying to kill him. He was not speaking metaphorically. Shortly, he came to believe the doctor had organized a vast conspiracy that was trying to destroy him. That obsessive belief in a conspiracy would remain with him. Two years later, when he was committed to a psychiatric facility, he would speak endlessly of how the doctor was behind everything that was happening to him. By that time, the doctor had retired. I did not have that option.

After several weeks in the health center, my father had enough control of the vertigo to return to his apartment. His new life now amounted to little more than sitting in a chair at his kitchen table. There, he would read the papers, listen to music, and occasionally watch television. He was reluctant to move. A walker appeared by his side; a wheelchair in the hallway. He became profoundly depressed.

He announced one day that he wanted to go to the hospice. We told him that he was not dying and that they would not take him. He insisted. We had to bring in a nurse from the hospice, who told him the same thing. He announced that he would stop eating and starve himself to death. He was, he said, going to "do a Gandhi." The suicidal impulse disappeared, after the doctor threatened to have him force-fed. My father, who had resisted doctors and drugs for decades, was now on antidepressants. The nurse would show up each evening and unlock a toolbox full of medications. I began to speak to doctors about his medication levels.

After the vertigo and the threats of suicide came the first hallucinations. He started seeing things or losing his vision, depending on what one made of his complaints. He became obsessive about cleaning his apartment and complained of dirt everywhere. When pressed, he would say it was not really dirt. It was, rather, masses of tiny spiders moving across his field of vision. I took him to an ophthalmologist. He thought that there was a physical cause of his vision problem, which could be cured with laser surgery. We went back for the operation and the effect was remarkable. Over the course of the visit, he went from being able only to read the largest letter on the chart to being able to read normally.

It did not last. Within days, he was complaining again of spiders. Now, they occupied only the lower portion of his vision. I would try to explain to him that they were not there. I would show him that by moving a blank piece of paper from the lower to the upper portions of his vision, the spiders disappeared. He was puzzled, but not convinced. I would tell him that I could only report what I saw and I saw no spiders.

He would rage at me, convinced I was lying or conspiring with others. He would tell me I should get my eyes checked. If we were on the phone, he would slam down the receiver. At times, he would tell me that he did not want to see me. Eventually, he learned not to complain about the spiders, since people told him he was seeing things. He feared being treated as psychotic. Every once in a while, he would check with me to see if I could now see the spiders. They literally haunted his vision. He now lived in a world of filth, with spiders crawling over the floors and up the walls. They got on his skin and he would scratch "the bites" until he bled. He was beyond help from an ophthalmologist.

By this time, he had a new companion. I was surprised that anyone would put up with him, but she did. Soon, however, he was again telling me things I did not want to hear about his disregard and disrespect for older women. She, nevertheless, sat by his side until the end. This despite her own ailments, which landed her too in the basement health center. In the last year of his life, they were both in the center, which was very fortunate for my father. Even when she was with him, however, there was little communication. He was increasingly lost in his own depression and obsessive rage.

The vertigo and the spiders were just the beginning. They were small episodes on the way to the disruption that was the last two years of his life. One winter morning, I again got a call from the health center. My father had been rushed out of the facility in an ambulance in the dead of night. He had been found in the hallway screaming that his apartment was full of dead chickens and occupied by strangers. A mother and two young girls were sitting on his couch. They sent him to the same local emergency room that I had often visited with my mother.

I found an unhappy scene when I arrived. No one on the staff knew what to do with him. They knew how to dress wounds and set broken bones. They were not set up for psychiatric care. They did not think it their responsibility to care for an elderly man having hallucinations. Remarkably, by the time I arrived, my father was speaking of the events of that night as a "psychotic episode." He knew something had happened and that he needed treatment. Unlike with the spiders, he could tell fact from fiction here.

While the local emergency facility did not want him, the assisted-living facility was not prepared to take him back. Eventually, a nurse found a space in the geriatric psychiatric facility attached to a large New Haven hospital. We thought we were lucky to get him a bed. That judgment was a mistake. My father's life would never be the same. The count of his final days began with arrival at the emergency entrance to the hospital.

I did not know at the time, but now I think we were sent to the emergency room because they needed a doctor formally to commit my father. He had not seen his personal doctor since the ambulance had taken him away in the night. We waited for hours in the psychiatric wing of the emergency department. All around us were the homeless and addicted. We did not understand what we were waiting for. We thought he was going to the psychiatric facility for assessment and evaluation. My siblings and I had long spoken about this possibility, but he had adamantly refused. Now, the psychotic episode gave us an opportunity. That, at least, is what we thought.

Eventually, he was assigned to a small room, in the emergency department. There, I began to understand what "psychiatric treatment" meant. The room had been stripped bare of any moveable objects. There was no door, no toilet seat, no phone, and no television remote. There was no way to control lights or noise. This bare room had been designed for just one purpose: to prevent suicide. I tried to explain that my father was not suicidal. He was seeing things; he was not threatening to kill himself.

I stayed into the night, but eventually went home to get some sleep. I thought he could survive one night there. When I returned in the morning, he was gone. Over the course of the night, he had been committed. I was more than a little surprised. No one had spoken to me, and I had the medical power of attorney. No one had asked if we would like to bring in his own doctor or a psychiatrist to do an evaluation. No one had asked for background information or had thought it necessary to find out what the family expected. In the emergency room, no one even bothered to explain to me what had happened. Indeed, it took me several days to learn that he had not just been transferred, but had been legally committed. This was against his will and without my consent. I still have no idea on what basis this decision was made or even who made it—a harried ER doctor in the middle of the night?

I found my father in the geriatric, psychiatric facility in a nearby building. It was clear from the start that they did not encourage visitors. To get in, I had to go through an elaborate procedure of signing in and removing everything I brought with me or carried in my pockets. He was in another bare room, with nothing to do. I could not bring him books, magazines, or music. They worried about staples in magazines and the hard edges of bookbindings. I offered to bring in a CD player. The staff told me he might strangle himself with the cord or slash his throat with a CD. I told them he was not suicidal. They said someone else might come into his room. I suggested it was their responsibility to keep patients out of each other's rooms and that doors might help.

He had no phone. The patients shared one portable phone. When I called, inevitably some other patient would answer and then immediately hang up after saying that my father was not there. The only entertainment was a large television constantly on in the common dining area. To my surprise, no one monitored what was on this television. Frequently, I saw scenes of violence and abuse.

All of this was about suicide; none of it was about evaluation or treatment. For the first three or four days he was there, he received no professional help at all. Each day, a different psychiatric social worker would check in, but do nothing. None of them spoke with me. It was a long weekend and there seemed to be no actual psychiatrists available. No one seemed to know why he was there or what to do with him. When I explained that he wanted to leave and I had not given permission, I was told that he could not leave. He was in a psychiatric gulag.

After the weekend, a psychiatrist did talk with him. When I requested to meet with her, I found that she had everything wrong. She had taken the word of a psychotic, hallucinating patient for the truth about his condition. She started telling me that he was suffering from loneliness because all of his children were away. She had no idea that his loneliness was of the existential sort and I had not been out of town. I spoke to her for more than two hours, by the end of which she concluded that he had Lewy Body dementia—a wasting illness for which there is no cure.

I could see no reason for him to be there. More importantly, he saw no reason why he was there. Nothing was being done for him. He moved from panic, to depression, to rage. He wanted out and he wanted it immediately. By the third day, he was in an uncontrollable rage, and I was at the center of it. He blamed me. I had put him there. I was colluding with the old doctor from the health center to have him imprisoned. If my mother had been the "fucking whore," I was now the "fucking son." He screamed, "How could you do this to me?" He asked, "What have I ever done to deserve this?" There was an answer to that question, but I kept silent.

He was there for twelve days. I spent my time outside of the hospital trying everything I could think of to get him released. I spoke to lawyers. I learned about Connecticut commitment procedures. I worked the phones with everyone I knew connected to the hospital. Eventually, I got through to the chief of staff who ordered a review. That finally led to his release.

In the first few days, I was allowed to visit him in his room. The staff must have decided his scenes of violent rage were upsetting to the other patients, for they banished me to the visitor's rooms on the other side of a locked door. They would try, not always successfully, to bring him out to see me. When he arrived, he would be furious. He would scream obscenities—more or less what he had said to my mother. If it were lunchtime, he would pick up a dish and threaten me with it. I would tell him that if he threw it, he would be committed for even longer. He would throw it down on his tray. As his furor grew, so did his obsession with the conspiracy. Sometimes, he would refuse to speak to me at all. He would sit looking at me with hatred and disgust. He heard everything I said as part of the cover up.

My father went into the hospital needing evaluation for a psychotic episode; he came out twelve days later broken, obsessive, and raging. On any scale of mental health, he had gone from the middle to the top of the chart. The psychiatric facility and its staff quite literally drove him crazy. My relationship to him never recovered.

He returned to the basement health center at the assisted-living community. I would visit him several times a week. I would cringe at the prospect, not knowing whom I would find. I would sit in my car in the parking lot, steeling my courage to go in. Often, he met me with rage, either screaming or refusing to speak. The conspiracy he imagined grew to include all of the doctors, nurses, and aides. They were stealing from him and plotting against him. He confused his time in the hospital with time in prison. He endlessly asked how I could do this to him.

He was on an ever-growing regime of drugs. These did subdue him, but it was entirely artificial. The health professionals actually had my father backwards. They thought the elderly person raging at the world was in the grip of illness. In fact, that was my father. The quiescent person they sought to create through pharmacological intervention was a ghost of that man. I cannot say, however, that they made the wrong choice. No one could live with his rage: not me, not the staff, and not even my father. He was breaking apart, while I was only miserable.

Soon enough, he was failing. He stopped eating regularly. He stopped doing much of anything. I would find him in his bed or a chair, simply staring into space. He was not thinking about the long course of his life. He was not remembering my mother or dreaming of his grandchildren. He was obsessing about his ill treatment. He felt hatred, full-on. There was no major episode; he simply slipped out of life one night.

My father had not one kind word to say before he died. He gave no blessings; he shared no insights. When he would get intolerably abusive, I would bring up my mother. I could not help myself. I thought sometimes that I could see a glimmer of recognition in his eyes—a fearful acknowledgment that I was right about his abuse and the pain he had caused. He would turn away, focusing instead on what I had done to him. He was sure to the end that he was the fuckee.

I told my father at the most painful moments that I was not his friend, that I had not forgiven him. I was taking responsibility as his son, but that was it. I had many occasions to think of what the doctor had told me, no one sticks to a person like my father. What was I doing there? Who gave him a pass on the responsibilities of a spouse or a father? Did he not have some responsibility to care for those around him?

A man who acts with such reckless disregard of the needs of others does not share the same earth with us. My father shared nothing with anybody, including his family. He deserved nothing from me or anyone else. Not from my mother, not from his final companions, and not from my siblings. He used and abused all those who would be close to him. Toward all of us, he had murder in his heart. I can try to explain him, but I cannot forgive him.

Why, then, did I not take the doctor's observation as a grant of permission to leave this man to whom I was never close? Having watched what he did to my mother, why did I allow myself to become his next victim? Was it that she and I both lacked the strength to walk away? I cannot say which—the decision to remain or to leave—would have required more strength. Surely, there was nothing easy about staying with him. In the end, I think the whole idea of making a decision is the wrong way to think about our moral life. Morality is not about choosing from a list of options. It is not about checking off the boxes or measuring possibilities against some abstract standard. I could not tally up my father's good and bad points on a scale to see which way the balance pointed.

We find ourselves in a world. We must make our way in that world as best we can, with whatever strength we can muster. We do right when we do our best to help those with whom we find ourselves flung together. We cannot make the world better wholesale, but we can try in the smaller circumstances that are our lot.

I thought of my father as the burden with which I was born. This was unfortunate, but it was also a part of who I am. I had to make my way in a world that included him. There was nothing right or wrong about this. It was unfortunate, but it was not unfair. We do not get to choose our world. The people who surround us are not ours to pick. In truth, we do not even pick our friends. We are thrown into common spaces with strangers in schools, on teams, in neighborhoods, and at work. Some of them become our friends. Perhaps new forms of social media are making it possible to choose our friends. I wonder what will happen to friendship if we take away from it the idea of fate. A friend by choice may be one that we easily leave by making a new choice. That, however, is not friendship at all.

If we are lucky, we fall in love with some of these people we find in our world. That too comes as if from nowhere. It is a blessing beyond our control; it is always more than we deserve. My wife and children are my good fortune; my father was my misfortune.

My father was part of my world and I could not walk away from him. I kept away as long as he did not need me. I was without the power to stay away, however, when he had the need. That responsibility was not diminished by his abuse. He was my problem to endure; he was my responsibility, not that of someone else. I had to help him even when he could not see the help. I never made excuses for him, although I often found myself apologizing for him.

I think that I did all right in the end. I certainly could have done better. I was never warm or tender toward him, but I do not think that he could have received this. We both knew that I did not love him. But then, we both also knew that he did not love me. He once loved my mother, but that was certainly the limit of his capacity for care. My mother's last words were of love. Those were words my father could not say and feelings he did not have. He did not want the support of love. He wanted the world not to be as it is.

At times, I hated my father. I hated what he had done to my mother; I hated the way he treated me. Nevertheless, I cared for him. When he died, I felt no sorrow, but only relief. I had no interest in memorializing him. I certainly had no interest in celebrating his life. I was at the event by the stream because my siblings wanted me there, but I would not add my voice. Yet, if this book finds readers, I will have managed to do just what I sought to avoid.

Difficult as he was, and as much as I struggled against him, this book is a kind of memorial to both my parents. When he died, I wanted him to make no lasting mark upon the world, but he has marked me. I cannot explain who I am or how I find a world of meaning in the midst of evil and distress without speaking of him. This is not a celebration of his life, but it is a reflection on it. To turn his rage into my thoughts is the final gift I have to give.

Killingworth, Connecticut, Summer 2020